THE TRANSFORMING POWER OF FAITH

POPE BENEDICT XVI

THE TRANSFORMING POWER OF FAITH

General Audiences

17 October 2012—6 February 2013

IGNATIUS PRESS   SAN FRANCISCO

English translation by *L'Osservatore Romano*

In Scripture references
chapter and verse numbering
may vary according
to the Bible version used

Cover Art
Christ Appears to the Apostles
after the Resurrection
(Panel from the Máesta Altarpiece)
Duccio di Buoninsegna (c.1260–1319)
Museo dell'Opera Metropolitana, Siena, Italy
©Scala/Art Resource, New York

Papal coat of arms image by www.AgnusImages.com

Cover design by Roxanne Mei Lum

© 2013 by Libreria Editrice Vaticana, Vatican City
Published in 2013 by Ignatius Press, San Francisco
ISBN 978-1-58617-842-0
Library of Congress Control Number 2013935554
Printed in the United States of America ⊗

CONTENTS

Introduction

WEDNESDAY, 17 OCTOBER 2012
Saint Peter's Square

Dear Brothers and Sisters,

Today I would like to introduce the new series of Catecheses that will develop throughout the Year of Faith that has just begun and will interrupt—during this period—the series on the school of prayer. I announced this special Year in the Apostolic Letter *Porta Fidei* precisely so that the Church might renew the enthusiasm of believing in Jesus Christ, the one Savior of the world, revive the joy of walking on the path he pointed out to us, and bear a tangible witness to the transforming power of faith.

The fiftieth anniversary of the opening of the Second Vatican Council is an important opportunity to return to God, to deepen our faith and live it more courageously, and to strengthen our belonging to the Church, "teacher of mankind". It is through the proclamation of the Word, the celebration of the sacraments, and works of charity that she guides us to meeting and knowing Christ, true God and true man. This is an encounter, not with an idea or with a project of life, but with a living Person who transforms our innermost selves, revealing to us our true identity as children of God. The encounter with Christ renews our human relationships, directing them, from day to day, to greater solidarity and brotherhood in the logic of love. Having faith in the Lord is not something that involves solely our intelligence, the area of intellectual knowledge; rather, it is a change that involves our life, our whole self: feelings, heart, intelligence, will, corporeity, emotions, and human relationships. With faith everything truly changes, in us and for us, and our future destiny is clearly revealed, the truth of our vocation in history, the meaning of life, the pleasure of being pilgrims bound for the heavenly homeland.

However—let us ask ourselves—is faith truly the transforming force in our life, in my life? Or is it merely one of the elements that are part of existence, without being the crucial one that involves it totally? With the Catecheses of this Year of Faith, let us make a journey to reinforce or rediscover the joy of faith, in the knowledge that it is not something extraneous, detached from daily life, but is its soul. Faith in a God who is love, who makes himself close to man by incarnating himself and by giving himself on the Cross, who saves us and opens the doors of Heaven to us once again, clearly indicates that man's fullness consists solely in love. This must be unequivocally reasserted today, when the cultural transformations under way frequently display so many forms of barbarity, passed off as "conquests of civilization". Faith affirms that there is no true humanity except in the places, actions, times, and forms in which man is motivated by the love that comes from God. It is expressed as a gift and reveals itself in relationships full of love, compassion, attention, and disinterested service to others. Wherever there is domination, possession, exploitation, and the taking advantage of the other for selfish reasons, wherever there is the arrogance of the ego withdrawn into the self, man is impoverished, debased, and disfigured. The Christian faith, active in charity and strong in hope, does not limit but rather humanizes life, indeed, makes it fully human.

Faith means taking this transforming message to heart in our life, receiving the Revelation of God, who makes us know that he exists, how he acts, and what his plans for us are. Of course, the mystery of God always remains beyond our conception and reason, our rites and our prayers. Yet, through his revelation, God actually communicates himself to us, recounts himself, and makes himself accessible. And we are enabled to listen to his Word and to receive his truth. This, then, is the wonder of faith: God, in his love, creates within us—through the action of the Holy Spirit—the appropriate conditions for us to recognize his Word. God himself, in his desire to show himself, to come into contact with us, to make himself present in our history, enables us to listen to and receive him. Saint Paul expresses it with joy and gratitude in these words: "And we also thank God constantly for this, that when you received the word of God which you heard from us, you accepted it not as the word of men but as what it really is, the word of God, which is at work in you believers" (1 Thess 2:13).

God has revealed himself with words and works throughout a long history of friendship with mankind, which culminated in the Incarnation of the Son of God and in the Mystery of his death and Resurrection. God not only revealed himself in the history of a people, he not only spoke through the Prophets, but he also crossed the threshold of his Heaven to enter our planet as a man, so that we might meet him and listen to him. And the proclamation of the Gospel of salvation spread from Jerusalem to the ends of the earth. The Church, born from Christ's side, became the messenger of a new and solid hope: Jesus of Nazareth Crucified and Risen, the Savior of the world, who is seated at the right hand of the Father and is the judge of the living and the dead. This is the kerygma, the central, explosive proclamation of faith. However, the problem of the "rule of faith" has been posed from the outset, in other words, the problem of believers' faithfulness to the truth of the Gospel, in which one must be firmly anchored, to the saving truth about God and man that must be preserved and passed down. Saint Paul wrote: "I preached to you the Gospel, which you received, in which you stand, by which you are saved, if you hold it fast—unless you believed in vain" (1 Cor 15:2).

But where can we find the essential formula of faith? Where can we find the truths that have been faithfully passed down to us and that constitute the light for our daily life? The answer is simple. In the Creed, in the Profession of Faith or Symbol of Faith, we are reconnected with the original event of the Person and history of Jesus of Nazareth; what the Apostle to the Gentiles said to the Christians of Corinth happens: "I delivered to you as of first importance what I also received, that Christ died for our sins in accordance with the Scriptures; that he was buried, that he was raised on the third day, in accordance with the Scriptures" (1 Cor 15:3–5).

Today, too, the Creed needs to be better known, understood, and prayed. It is important above all that the Creed be, so to speak, "recognized". Indeed, knowing might be merely an intellectual operation, whereas "recognizing" means the need to discover the deep bond between the truth we profess in the Creed and our daily existence, so that these truths may truly and in practice be—as they have always been—light for our steps through life, water that irrigates the parched stretches on our path, life that overcomes certain deserts of contemporary life. The moral life

of Christians is grafted on the Creed, on which it is founded
and by which it is justified.

It is not by chance that Blessed John Paul II wanted the
Catechism of the Catholic Church, a reliable norm for teaching the faith and a dependable source for a renewed catechesis, to be based on the Creed. It was a question of
confirming and preserving this central core of the truths of
the faith and of rendering it in a language that would be
more comprehensible to the people of our time, to us. It is
a duty of the Church to transmit the faith, to communicate
the Gospel, so that the Christian truths may be a light in
the new cultural transformations and that Christians may
be able to account for the hope that is in them (cf. 1 Pet
3:15). Today we are living in a society in constant move-
ment, one that has changed radically, even in comparison
with the recent past. The processes of secularization and a
widespread nihilistic mentality in which all is relative have
deeply marked the common mind-set. Thus life is often
lived frivolously, with no clear ideals or well-founded hopes
and within fluid and temporary social ties. Above all, the
new generations are not taught the truth or the profound
meaning of existence that surmounts the contingent situation or permanent affections and trust. Relativism leads, on
the contrary, to having no reference points, suspicion and
volubility break up human relations, while life is lived in
brief experiments without the assumption of responsibility.
If individualism and relativism seem to dominate the minds
of many of our contemporaries, it cannot be said that believers are completely immune to these dangers, with which
we are confronted in the transmission of the faith. The inves-
tigation promoted on all the continents through the celebration of the Synod of Bishops on the New Evangelization
has highlighted some of them: a faith lived passively and

privately, the rejection of education in the faith, the gap between life and faith.

Christians often do not even know the central core of their own Catholic faith, the Creed, so that they leave room for a certain syncretism and religious relativism, blurring the truths to believe in as well as the salvific uniqueness of Christianity. The risk of fabricating, as it were, a "do-it-yourself" religion is not so far off today. Instead we must return to God, to the God of Jesus Christ; we must rediscover the Gospel message and make it enter our consciences and our daily life more deeply.

In the Catecheses of this Year of Faith, I would like to offer some help for achieving this journey, for taking up and deepening knowledge of the central truths of our faith about God, man, the Church, about the whole social and cosmic reality, by meditating and reflecting on the affirmations of the Creed. And I would like it to be clear that this content or truth of faith (*fides quae*) bears directly on our life; it asks for a conversion of life that gives life to a new way of believing in God (*fides qua*). Knowing God, meeting him, deepening our knowledge of the features of his face is vital for our life so that he may enter into the profound dynamics of man.

May the journey we shall be making this year enable us all to grow in faith, in love of Christ, so that in our daily decisions and actions we may learn to live the good and beautiful life of the Gospel.

2

What Is Faith?

WEDNESDAY, 24 OCTOBER 2012
Saint Peter's Square

Dear Brothers and Sisters,

Last Wednesday, with the beginning of the Year of Faith, I started a new series of Catecheses on faith. And today I would like to reflect with you on a fundamental question: What is faith? Does faith still make sense in a world in which science and technology have unfolded horizons unthinkable until a short time ago? What does believing mean today? In fact, in our time we need a renewed education in the faith that includes, of course, knowledge of its truths and of the history of salvation but that is born above all from a true encounter with God in Jesus Christ, from loving him, from trusting him, so that the whole of our life becomes involved.

Today, together with so many signs of goodness, a certain spiritual desert is also developing around us. At times we almost have the feeling, from certain events we have news of every day, that the world is not moving toward the building of a more brotherly and peaceful community; the very ideas of progress and well-being have shadows, too. Despite the greatness of scientific discoveries and technological triumphs, men today do not seem to have become truly any freer or more human; so many forms of exploitation, manipulation, violence, abuse, and injustice endure.... A certain kind of culture, moreover, has taught people to move solely within the horizon of things, of the feasible, to believe only in what they can see and touch with their own hands. Yet the number is also growing of those who feel bewildered and, in seeking to go beyond a merely horizontal view of reality, are prepared to believe in everything and nothing. In this context, certain fundamental questions reemerge that are far weightier than they seem at first sight. What is life's meaning? Is there a future for mankind, for us and for the generations to come? In which direction should we orient our free decisions for a good and successful outcome in life? What awaits us beyond the threshold of death?

From these irrepressible questions it becomes clear how the world of planning, of precise calculation, and of experimentation, in a word, the knowledge of science, although important for human life, is not enough on its own. We do not only need bread, we need love, meaning, and hope, a sound foundation, a solid terrain that helps us to live with an authentic meaning even in times of crisis, in darkness, in difficulty, and with our daily problems. Faith gives us precisely this: it is a confident entrustment to a "You", who is God, who gives me a different certitude, but one that is no less solid than that which comes from precise calculation or from science. Faith is not a mere intellectual assent of the human person to specific truths about God; it is an act with which I entrust myself freely to a God who is Father and who loves me; it is adherence to a "You" who gives me hope and trust. Of course, this adherence to God is not without content; with it we are aware that God has shown himself to us in Christ, he has made us see his face and has made himself really close to each one of us. Indeed,

God has revealed that his love for man, for each one of us, is boundless: on the Cross, Jesus of Nazareth, the Son of God made man, shows us in the clearest possible way how far this love reaches, even to the gift of himself, even to the supreme sacrifice. With the mystery of Christ's death and Resurrection, God plumbs to the depths of our humanity to bring it back to him, to lift it up to his heights. Faith is believing in this love of God that is never lacking in the face of human wickedness, in the face of evil and death, but is capable of transforming every kind of slavery, giving us the possibility of salvation. Having faith, then, is meeting this "You", God, who supports me and grants me the promise of an indestructible love that not only aspires to eternity but gives it; it means entrusting myself to God with the attitude of a child, who knows well that all his difficulties, all his problems are understood in the "you" of his mother. And this possibility of salvation through faith is a gift that God offers all men. I think we should meditate more often—in our daily life, marked by problems and at times by dramatic situations—on the fact that believing in a Christian manner means my trusting abandonment to the profound meaning that sustains me and the world, that meaning which we are unable to give to each other but can only receive as a gift and which is the foundation on which we can live without fear. And we must be able to proclaim this liberating and reassuring certainty of faith with words and show it by living our life as Christians.

However, we see around us every day that many remain indifferent or refuse to accept this proclamation. At the end of Mark's Gospel, we heard harsh words from the Risen One, who says: "He who believes and is baptized will be saved; but he who does not believe will be condemned" (Mk 16:16), he loses himself. I would like to invite you to reflect on this. Trust in the action of the Holy Spirit must always impel us to go and preach the Gospel, to the courageous witness of faith; but, in addition to the possibility of making a positive response to the gift of faith, there is also the risk of rejecting the Gospel, of not accepting the vital encounter with Christ. Saint Augustine was already posing this problem in one of his commentaries on the Parable of the Sower. "We speak", he said, "we cast the seed, we scatter the seed. There are those who deride us, those who reproach us, those who mock at us. If we fear them, we have nothing left to sow, and on the day of reaping we will be left without a harvest. Therefore, may the seed in the good soil sprout" (*Discourse on Christian Discipline* 13, 14: PL 40, 677–78). Rejection, therefore, cannot discourage us. As Christians we are evidence of this fertile ground. Our faith, even with our limitations, shows that good soil exists, where the seed of the Word of God produces abundant fruits of justice, peace, and love, of new humanity, of salvation. And the whole history of the Church, with all the problems, also shows that good soil exists, that the good seed exists and bears fruit.

Yet, let us ask ourselves: Where can man find that openness of heart and mind to believe in God, who made himself visible in Jesus Christ, who died and rose, in order to receive God's salvation so that Christ and his Gospel might be the guide and the light of our existence? The answer: We can believe in God because he comes close to us and touches us, because the Holy Spirit, a gift of the Risen One, enables us to receive the living God. Thus faith is first of all a supernatural gift, a gift of God. The Second Vatican Council says: "Before this faith can be exercised, man must have the grace of God to move and assist him; he must have the interior help of the Holy Spirit, who moves the heart and converts it to God, who opens the eyes of the mind and 'makes it easy for all to accept and believe the truth'" (Dogmatic Constitution on Divine Revelation, *Dei Verbum*, no. 5). Our journey starts from Baptism, the sacrament that gives us the Holy Spirit, making us become children of God in Christ, and that marks our entry into the community of faith, into the Church: one does not believe by oneself, without the prior intervention of the grace of the Holy Spirit; one does not believe alone but, rather, together with one's brethren. From Baptism every believer is called to live a new life and to make this confession of faith his own, together with the brethren.

Faith is a gift of God, but it is also a profoundly free and human act. The *Catechism of the Catholic Church* says so clearly: "Believing is possible only by grace and the interior helps of the Holy Spirit. But it is no less true that believing is an authentically human act ... contrary neither to human freedom nor to human reason" (no. 154). Indeed, it involves them and lifts them up in a gamble for life that is like an exodus, that is, a coming out of ourselves, from our own certainties, from our own mental framework, to entrust ourselves to the action of God, who points out to us his way to achieve true freedom, our human identity, true joy of the heart, peace with everyone. Believing means entrusting oneself in full freedom and joyfully to God's providential plan for history, as did the Patriarch Abraham, as did Mary of Nazareth. Faith, then, is an assent with which our mind and our heart say their "yes" to God, confessing that Jesus is Lord. And this "yes" transforms life, unfolds the path toward fullness of meaning, thereby making it new, rich in joy and trustworthy hope.

Dear friends, our time needs Christians who have been grasped by Christ, who grow in faith through their familiarity with Sacred Scripture and the sacraments. People who are, as it were, an open book that tells of the experience of new life in the Spirit, of the presence of that God who supports us on our way and opens us to everlasting life.

3

The Faith of the Church

WEDNESDAY, 31 OCTOBER 2012
Saint Peter's Square

Dear Brothers and Sisters,

Let us continue on our journey of meditations on the Catholic faith. Last week I showed how faith is a gift, because it is God who takes the initiative and comes to meet us, and, thus, faith is an answer by which we receive him as the permanent foundation of our life. It is a gift that changes our existence, because it makes us enter into Jesus' own vision, which works in us and opens us to love for God and for others.

Today I would like to take another step in our reflection, starting once more with a few questions: Does faith have a solely personal, individual nature? Does it concern only myself? Do I live my faith alone? Of course, the act of faith is an eminently personal act; it happens in the deepest part of us and signals a change in direction through personal conversion. It is my life that changes, that is given a new direction. In the Rite of Baptism, at the moment of the promises, the celebrant asks for a profession of the Catholic faith and formulates three questions: Do you believe in God the Father Almighty? Do you believe in Jesus Christ his only Son? Do you believe in the Holy Spirit? In ancient times these questions were addressed to the person who was to receive Baptism before being immersed three times in water. And today, too, the answer is one and the same: "I do". But this faith of mine is not the result of my own solitary reflection, it is not the product of my thought; it is the fruit of a relationship, a dialogue, in which there is a listener, a receiver, and a respondent; it is communication with Jesus that draws me out of the "I" enclosed in myself to open me to the love of God, the Father. It is like a rebirth in which I am united not only to Jesus, but also to all those who have walked and are walking on the same path; and this new birth that begins with Baptism continues for the rest of my life. I cannot build my personal faith in a private dialogue with Jesus, because faith is given to me by God through a community of believers that is the Church and projects me into the multitude of believers, into a kind of communion that is not only sociological but rooted in the eternal love of God, who is in himself the communion of the Father and of the Son and of the Holy Spirit, it is Trinitarian Love. Our faith is truly personal only if it is also communal: it can be my faith only if it dwells in and moves with the "we" of the Church, only if it is our faith, the common faith of the one Church.

On Sunday, in the Holy Mass, reciting the "Creed", we speak in the first person, but we confess as one the one faith of the Church. That "I believe" said individually joins a vast chorus across time and space, in which each person contributes, so to speak, to the harmonious polyphony in faith. The *Catechism of the Catholic Church* sums this up in a clear way: "'Believing' is an ecclesial act. The Church's faith precedes, engenders, supports, and nourishes our faith. The Church is the mother of all believers. 'No one can have God as Father who does not have the Church as Mother'

(St. Cyprian)" (no. 181). Therefore, the faith is born in the Church, leads to her, and lives in her. This is important to remember.

At the start of the Christian adventure, when the Holy Spirit descends with power upon the disciples, on the day of Pentecost—as we read in the Acts of the Apostles (cf. 2:1–13)—the early Church receives the power to begin the mission entrusted to her by the Risen Lord: to spread the Gospel to every corner of the earth, the Good News of the Kingdom of God, and thus to lead every man to the encounter with him, to the faith that saves. The Apostles overcome every fear in proclaiming what they have heard, seen, personally experienced with Jesus. By the power of the Holy Spirit, they start to speak in tongues, openly announcing the mystery of which they were witnesses. In the Acts of the Apostles, we are told then of the great discourse that Peter gives on the day of Pentecost. He begins with a passage from the Prophet Joel (3:1–5), referring to Jesus and proclaiming the central nucleus of the Christian faith: The One who had benefited all, who had been attested to by God with mighty works, wonders, and signs, was nailed to the Cross and killed, but God raised him from the dead, making him Lord and Christ. With him we have come into the ultimate salvation foretold by the Prophets, and whoever invokes his name will be saved (cf. Acts 2:17–24). Listening to these words of Peter, many felt called personally, repented of their sins, and were baptized, receiving the gift of the Holy Spirit (cf. Acts 2:37–41). And so began the journey of the Church, the community that bears this proclamation through time and space, the community that is the People of God founded on the New Covenant thanks to the Blood of Christ. Her members do not belong to a particular social or ethnic group, but are men and women of every nation and culture. It is a "catholic" people, a people who speaks in tongues, universally open to welcoming all, beyond all boundaries, breaking down every barrier. Saint Paul says: "Here there cannot be Greek and Jew, circumcised and uncircumcised, barbarian, Scythian, slave, free man, but Christ is all, and in all" (Col 3:11).

The Church, therefore, from the beginning is the place of faith, the place for the transmission of the faith, the place in which, through Baptism, we are immersed in the Paschal Mystery of the death and Resurrection of Christ, who frees us from the slavery of sin, gives us the freedom of children, and introduces us into communion with the Trinitarian God. At the same time, we are immersed in communion with other brothers and sisters of the faith, with the entire Body of Christ, brought out of our isolation. The Second Vatican Ecumenical Council reminds us: "God, however, does not make men holy and save them merely as individuals, without bond or link between one another. Rather has it pleased Him to bring men together as one people, a people which acknowledges Him in truth and serves Him in holiness" (cf. Dogmatic Constitution *Lumen Gentium*, no. 9). Referring back again to the Rite of Baptism, we note that, at the end of the promises in which we voice our renunciation of evil and repeat "I believe" to the truths of the faith, the celebrant declares: "This is our faith. This is the faith of the Church. We are proud to profess it, in Christ Jesus our Lord." Faith is a theological virtue, given by God, but transmitted by the Church throughout history. Saint Paul himself, writing to the Corinthians, affirms he has communicated to them the Gospel that he, too, had received (cf. 1 Cor 15:3).

There is an unbroken chain in the life of the Church, in the proclamation of the Word of God, in the celebration of the sacraments, that has come down to us and that we call Tradition. It gives us the guarantee that what we believe is the original message of Christ, preached by the Apostles. The nucleus of the primordial proclamation is the death and the Resurrection of the Lord, from which stems the entire patrimony of the faith. The Council says: "The apostolic preaching, which is expressed in a special way in the inspired books, was to be preserved by an unending succession of preachers until the end of time" (Dogmatic Constitution *Dei Verbum*, no. 8). In this way, if Sacred Scripture contains the Word of God, the Tradition of the Church preserves it and faithfully transmits it, so that the men of every age might have access to its vast resources and be enriched by its treasures of grace. Thus, the Church, "in her doctrine, life and worship, perpetuates and transmits to every generation all that she herself is, all that she believes" (*ibid.*).

Lastly, I would like to emphasize that it is in the ecclesial community that personal faith grows and matures. It is interesting to observe how in the New Testament the word "saints" designates Christians as a whole, and certainly not all would have qualified to be declared saints by the Church. What is meant, then, by this term? The fact that whoever had and lived the faith in Christ Risen was called to become a point of reference for all others, setting them in this way in contact with the Person and the Message of Jesus, who reveals the face of the Living God. And this holds true also for us: a Christian who lets himself be guided and gradually shaped by the faith of the Church, in spite of his weaknesses, his limitations, and his difficulties, becomes like a window open to the light of the living God, receiving this light and transmitting it to the world. Blessed John Paul II in his Encyclical *Redemptoris Missio* declared that "missionary activity renews the Church, revitalizes faith and Christian identity, and offers fresh enthusiasm and new incentive. Faith is strengthened when it is given to others" (no. 2).

Today's widespread tendency to relegate faith to the private sphere thus contradicts its very nature. We need the Church in order to confirm our faith and in order to experience the gifts of God: his Word, the sacraments, the support of grace, and the witness of love. Thus, our "I" can be perceived in the "we" of the Church and, at the same time, be the recipient and the protagonist of an overwhelming event: experiencing communion with God, which is the foundation of communion among men. In a world in which individualism seems to rule personal relationships, making them ever more fragile, the faith calls us to be the People of God, to be Church, bearers of the love and communion of God for all mankind (cf. Pastoral Constitution *Gaudium et Spes*, no. 1).

4

The Desire for God

WEDNESDAY, 7 NOVEMBER 2012
Saint Peter's Square

Dear Brothers and Sisters,

The journey of reflection that we are making together during this Year of Faith leads us to meditate today on a fascinating aspect of the human and the Christian experience: man carries within himself a mysterious desire for God. In a very significant way, the *Catechism of the Catholic Church* opens precisely with the following consideration: "The desire for God is written in the human heart, because man is created by God and for God; and God never ceases to draw man to himself. Only in God will he find the truth and happiness he never stops searching for" (no. 27).

A statement like this, which even today in many cultural contexts seems quite acceptable, even obvious, might, however, be taken as a provocation in the West's secularized culture. Many of our contemporaries might actually object that they have no such desire for God. For large sectors of society, he is no longer the one longed for or desired but rather a reality that leaves them indifferent, one on which there is no need even to comment. In reality, what we have defined as "the desire for God" has not entirely disappeared, and it still appears today, in many ways, in the heart of man. Human desire always tends toward certain concrete goods, often anything but spiritual, and yet it has to face the question of what is truly "the" good and, thus, is confronted with something other than itself, something man cannot build but is called to recognize. What can really satisfy man's desire?

In my first Encyclical, *Deus Caritas Est*, I sought to analyze the way in which this dynamism can be found in the experience of human love, an experience that in our age is more easily perceived as a moment of ecstasy, of leaving oneself, like a place in which man feels overcome by a desire that surpasses him. Through love, a man and a woman experience in a new way, thanks to each other, the greatness and beauty of life and of what is real. If what is experienced is not a mere illusion, if I truly want the good of the other as a means for my own good, then I must be willing not to be self-centered, to place myself at the other's service, even to the point of self-denial. The answer to the question on the meaning of the experience of love then passes through the purification and healing of the will, required in loving the other. We must cultivate, encourage, and also correct ourselves, so that this good can truly be willed.

Thus the initial ecstasy becomes a pilgrimage, "an ongoing exodus out of the closed inward-looking self towards its liberation through self-giving, and thus towards authentic self-discovery and indeed the discovery of God" (Encyclical *Deus Caritas Est*, no. 6). Through this journey one will be able to deepen gradually one's knowledge of that love, initially experienced. And the mystery that it represents will become more and more defined: in fact, not even the beloved is capable of satisfying the desire that dwells in the human heart. Rather, the more authentic one's love for the other is, the more it reveals the question of its origin and its destiny, of the possibility that it may endure forever. Therefore, the human experience of love has in itself a dynamism that refers beyond oneself, it is the experience of a good that leads one to go out of oneself and find oneself before the mystery that encompasses the whole of existence.

One could make similar observations about other human experiences as well, such as friendship, encountering beauty, loving knowledge: every good experienced by man projects him toward the mystery that surrounds man himself; every desire that springs up in the human heart echoes a fundamental desire that is never fully satisfied. Undoubtedly from that deep desire, which also contains something enigmatic, one cannot arrive directly at faith. Man, after all, knows well what does not satisfy him, but he cannot imagine or define what the happiness he longs for in his heart would be like. One cannot know God based on human desire alone. From this point of view, he remains a mystery: man is the seeker of the Absolute, seeking with small and hesitant steps. And yet, already the experience of desire, of a "restless heart", as Saint Augustine called it, is very meaningful. It tells us that man is, deep down, a religious being (cf. the *Catechism of the Catholic Church*, no. 28), a "beggar before God". We can say with the words of Pascal: "Man infinitely surpasses man" (*Pensées*, ed. Chevalier 438; ed. Brunschvicg 434). Eyes recognize things when they are illuminated. From this comes a desire to know the light itself, what makes the things of the world shine and with them ignites the sense of beauty.

We must, therefore, maintain that it is possible also in this age, seemingly so blocked to the transcendent dimension, to begin a journey toward the true religious meaning of life that shows how the gift of faith is not senseless, is not irrational. It would be very useful, to that end, to foster a kind of pedagogy of desire, both for the journey of one who does not yet believe and for the one who has already received the gift of faith. It should be a pedagogy that covers at least two aspects. In the first place, to discover or rediscover the taste of the authentic joy of life. Not all satisfactions have the same effect on us: some leave a positive aftertaste, able to calm the soul and make us more active and generous. Others, however, after the initial delight, seem to disappoint the expectations that they have awakened and sometimes leave behind them a sense of bitterness, dissatisfaction, or emptiness. Instilling in someone from a young age the taste for true joy, in every area of life—family, friendship, solidarity with those who suffer, self-renunciation for the sake of the other, love of knowledge, art, the beauty of nature—all this means exercising the inner taste and producing effective antibodies against today's widespread trivialization and dulling. Adults, too, need to rediscover this joy, to desire authenticity, to purify themselves of the mediocrity that might infest them. It will then become easier to drop or reject everything that although attractive proves to be, in fact, insipid, a source of indifference and not of freedom. And this will bring out that desire for God of which we are speaking.

A second aspect that goes hand in hand with the preceding one is never to be content with what you have achieved. It is precisely the truest joy that unleashes in us the healthy restlessness that leads us to be more demanding—to want a higher good, a deeper good—and at the same time to perceive ever more clearly that no finite thing can fill our heart. In this way, we will learn to strive, unarmed, for the good that we cannot build or attain by our own power; and we will learn not to be discouraged by the difficulty or the obstacles that come from our sin.

In this regard, we must not forget that the dynamism of desire is always open to redemption. Even when it strays from the path, when it follows artificial paradises and seems to lose the capacity to yearn for the true good. Even in the abyss of sin, that ember is never fully extinguished in man. It allows him to recognize the true good, to savor it, and thus to start out again on a path of ascent; God, by the gift of his grace, never denies man his help. We all, moreover, need to set out on the path of purification and healing of desire. We are pilgrims, heading for the heavenly homeland, toward that full and eternal good that nothing will be able to take away from us. This is not, then, about suffocating the longing that dwells in the heart of man, but about freeing it, so that it can reach its true height. When in desire one opens the window to God, this is already a sign of the presence of faith in the soul, faith that is a grace of God. Saint Augustine always says: "So God, by deferring our hope, stretches our desire; by the desiring, stretches the mind; by stretching, makes it more capacious" (*Commentary on the First Letter of John* 4, 6: PL 35, 2009).

On this pilgrimage, let us feel like brothers of all men, traveling companions even of those who do not believe, of those who are seeking, of those who are sincerely wondering about the dynamism of their own aspiration for the true and the good. Let us pray, in this Year of Faith, that God may show his face to all those who seek him with a sincere heart.

5

The Ways That Lead to
Knowledge of God

WEDNESDAY, 14 NOVEMBER 2012
Paul VI Audience Hall

Dear Brothers and Sisters,

Last Wednesday we reflected on the desire for God that man carries deep within himself. Today I would like to continue to examine this aspect, meditating briefly with you on some of the ways to attain knowledge of God. I wish to recall, however, that God's initiative always precedes every human initiative, and on our journey toward him, too, it is he who first illuminates us, who directs and guides us, ever respecting our inner freedom. It is always he who admits us to intimacy with himself, revealing himself and giving us the grace to be able to accept this revelation in faith. Let us never forget Saint Augustine's experience: it is not we who possess the Truth after having sought it, but the Truth that seeks us out and possesses us.

Nonetheless, there are ways that can open the human heart to knowledge of God, there are signs that lead to God. Of course, we often risk being dazzled by the glare of worldliness that makes us less able to follow these paths and to read these signs. Yet God never tires of seeking us; he is faithful to man, whom he created and redeemed; he stays close to us in our life because he loves us. This is a certainty that must accompany us every day, even if a certain widespread mentality makes it harder for the Church and for Christians to communicate to every creature the joy of the Gospel and to lead everyone to the encounter with Jesus, the one Savior of the world. However, this is our mission. It is the mission of the Church, and every believer must carry it out joyously, feeling it his own, through an existence truly enlivened by faith, marked by charity, by service to God and to others, and capable of radiating hope. This mission shines out above all in the holiness to which we are all called.

Today—as we know—faith, which is all too often not properly understood and contested or rejected, encounters no lack of difficulties and trials. Saint Peter said to his Christians: "Always be prepared to make a defense to any one who calls you to account for the hope that is in you, yet do it with gentleness and reverence" (1 Pt 3:15). In the past, in the West, in a society deemed Christian, faith was the context in which people acted; reference and adherence to God were part of daily life for the majority. Rather, it was the person who did not believe who had to justify his own incredulity. In our world, the situation has changed, and, increasingly, it is believers who must be able to account for their faith. In his Encyclical *Fides et Ratio*, Blessed John Paul II stressed that faith is also put to the test in our day, riddled with subtle and captious forms of atheism, both theoretical and practical (cf. nos. 46–47). Ever since the Enlightenment, the criticism of religion has been gathering momentum; history has also come to be marked by the presence of atheistic systems in which God was seen as a mere projection of the human mind, an illusion and the product of a society already misled by so many alienating factors. Moreover, the past century experienced a strong process of secularization under the banner of the absolute autonomy of man, considered as the measure and architect of reality, but impoverished by being created "in the image and likeness of God". A particularly dangerous phenomenon for faith has arisen in our times: indeed, a form of atheism exists which we define, precisely, as "practical", in which the truths of faith or religious rites are not denied but are merely deemed irrelevant to daily life, detached from life, pointless. So it is that people often believe in God in a superficial manner and live "as though God did not exist" (*etsi Deus non daretur*). In the end, however, this way of life proves even more destructive because it leads to indifference to faith and to the question of God.

In fact, man, separated from God, is reduced to a single dimension—the horizontal—and this reductionism itself is one of the fundamental causes of the various forms of totalitarianism that have had tragic consequences in the past century as well as of the crisis of values that we see in the current situation. By obscuring the reference to God, the ethical horizon has also been obscured, in order to leave room for relativism and for an ambiguous conception of freedom which, instead of being liberating, ends by binding men to idols. The temptations that Jesus faced in the wilderness before his public ministry vividly symbolize those "idols" which entice man when he does not go beyond himself. Were God to lose his centrality, man would lose his rightful place, he would no longer fit into creation, into relations with others. What ancient wisdom evokes with the myth of Prometheus has not faded: man thinks he himself can become a "god", master of life and death.

With this picture before her, the Church, faithful to Christ's mandate, never ceases to affirm the truth about man and about his destiny. The Second Vatican Council affirms it concisely: "The dignity of man rests above all on the fact that he is called to communion with God. The invitation to converse with God is addressed to man as soon as he comes into being. For if man exists, it is because God has created him through love and, through love, continues to hold him in existence. He cannot live fully according to truth unless he freely acknowledges that love and unless he entrusts himself to his Creator" (Pastoral Constitution on the Church in the Modern World, *Gaudium et Spes*, no. 19).

What answers, therefore, is faith required to give, "with gentleness and reverence", to atheism, to scepticism, to indifference to the vertical dimension, in order that the people of our time may continue to ponder on the existence of God and take paths that lead to him? I want to point out several paths that derive both from natural reflection and from the power of faith itself. I would like to sum them up very briefly in three words: the world, man, faith.

The first word: the world. Saint Augustine, who spent much of his life seeking the Truth and was grasped by the Truth, wrote a very beautiful and famous passage in which he said: "Question the beauty of the earth, question the beauty of the sea, question the beauty of the air distending and diffusing itself, question the beauty of the sky ... question all these realities. All respond: 'See, we are beautiful.' Their beauty is a profession [*confessio*]. These beauties are subject to change. Who made them if not the Beautiful One [*Pulcher*] who is not subject to change?" (*Sermo* 241, 2: PL 38, 1134). I think we should recover—and enable people today to recover—our capacity for contemplating creation, its beauty and its structure. The world is not a shapeless mass of magma, but the better we know it and the better we discover its marvelous mechanisms, the more clearly we can see a plan, we see that there is a creative intelligence. Albert Einstein said that in natural law is revealed "an intelligence of such superiority that, compared with it, all the systematic thinking and acting of human beings is an utterly insignificant reflection" (*The World As I See It*, 1949). Consequently, a first path that leads to the discovery of God is an attentive contemplation of creation.

The second word: man. Again, Saint Augustine was to write a famous sentence in which he says that God is more intimate to me than I am to myself (cf. *Confessions* III, 6, 11). Hence he formulates the invitation: "Do not go outside yourself, return to yourself: the truth is higher than my highest and more inward than my innermost self" (*De Vera Religione* 39, 72). This is another aspect that we risk losing in the noisy and dispersive world in which we live: the ability to pause and look deeply into ourselves and to reinterpret the thirst for the infinite that we bear within us, that impels us to go farther and to refer to the One who can quench it. The *Catechism of the Catholic Church* says: "With his openness to truth and beauty, his sense of moral goodness, his freedom and the voice of his conscience, with his longings for the infinite and for happiness, man questions himself about God's existence" (no. 33).

The third word: faith. We must not forget, especially in the situation of our time, that the life of faith is a path which leads to the knowledge of and encounter with God. Those who believe are united to God and open to his grace, to the power of his love. Thus their existence becomes a witness, not of themselves, but of the Risen One, and their faith does not hesitate to shine out in daily life, open to dialogue that expresses deep friendship for the journey of every man and can bring hope to people in need of redemption, happiness, a future. Faith, in fact, is an encounter with God who speaks and works in history and converts our daily life, transforming within us mentalities, value judgments, decisions, and practical actions. Faith is not an illusion, a flight of fancy, a refuge, or sentimentalism; rather, it is total involvement in the whole of life and is the proclamation of the Gospel, the Good News that can set the whole man free. A Christian and a community that are active and faithful to the plan of God, who loved us first, are privileged paths for those immersed in indifference or in doubt about their life and action. However, this asks each and every one to make his testimony of faith ever more transparent, purifying his life so that it may be in conformity with Christ. Many people today have a limited idea of the Christian faith, because they identify it with a mere system of beliefs and values rather than with the truth of a God who revealed himself in history, anxious to communicate with man personally, in a relationship of love with him. In fact, at the root of every doctrine or value is the event of the encounter between man and God in Jesus Christ. Christianity, before being a moral or an ethic, is the event of love, it is the acceptance of the Person of Jesus. For this reason, the Christian and Christian communities must first look and make others look to Christ, the true Way that leads to God.

6

The Reasonableness of Faith in God

WEDNESDAY, 21 NOVEMBER 2012
Paul VI Audience Hall

Dear Brothers and Sisters,

Let us proceed in this Year of Faith bearing in our hearts the hope of finding all the joy there is in believing and of rediscovering the enthusiasm of communicating the truths of the faith to all. These truths are not a simple message about God, a particular piece of information about him. On the contrary, they express the event of God's encounter with man, a salvific and liberating encounter which fulfills the deepest aspirations of the human heart, the yearning for peace, brotherhood, and love. Faith leads to the discovery that the meeting with God enhances, perfects, and exalts all that is true, good, and beautiful that exists in man. So it happens that while God reveals himself and lets himself be known, man comes to realize who God is and, in knowing him, discovers himself, his true origin, his destiny, the greatness and dignity of human life.

Faith makes possible authentic knowledge about God, which involves the whole man: it is a "sapere", that is, a knowledge which gives life a savor, a new taste, a joyful way of being in the world. Faith is expressed in the gift of self for others, in brotherhood which creates solidarity, the ability to love, overcoming the loneliness that brings sadness. Thus this knowledge of God through faith is not only intellectual but also vital. It is the knowledge of God-Love, thanks to his own love. The love of God, moreover, makes us see, opens our eyes, enables us to know the whole of reality, in addition to the narrow views of individualism and subjectivism that confuse consciences. Knowledge of God is therefore an experience of faith and at the same time entails an intellectual and moral development; moved in our depths by the Spirit of Jesus within us, we go beyond the horizons of our own selfishness and open ourselves to the true values of existence.

Today, in this Catechesis, I would like to reflect on the reasonableness of faith in God. The Catholic Tradition, from the outset, rejected so-called "fideism", which is the desire to believe against reason. *Credo quia absurdum* (I believe because it is absurd) is not a formula that interprets the Catholic faith. Indeed, God is not absurd; if anything, he is a mystery. The mystery, in its turn, is not irrational but is a superabundance of sense, of meaning, of truth. If, looking at the mystery, reason sees darkness, it is not because there is no light in the mystery but, rather, because there is too much of it. Just as when men raise their eyes to look at the sun, they are blinded; but who would say that the sun is not bright or, indeed, the fount of light? Faith permits us to look at the "sun", God, because it is the acceptance of his Revelation in history and, so to speak, the true reception of God's mystery, recognizing the great miracle. God came close to man, he offered himself so that man might know him, stooping to the creaturely limitations of human reason (cf. Second Vatican Ecumenical Council, Dogmatic Constitution, *Dei Verbum*, no. 13). At the same time, God, with his grace, illuminates reason, unfolds new horizons before it, boundless and infinite. For this reason, faith is an incentive to seek always, never to stop and never to be content in the inexhaustible search for truth and reality. The prejudice of certain modern thinkers, who hold that human reason would be, as it were, blocked by the dogmas of faith, is false. Exactly the opposite is true, as the great teachers of the Catholic Tradition have shown. Saint Augustine, before his conversion, sought the Truth with great restlessness through all the philosophies he had at his disposal, finding them all unsatisfactory. His demanding, rational search was a meaningful pedagogy for him for the encounter with the Truth of Christ. When he says: "I believe in order to understand, and I understand the better to believe" (*Discourse* 43, 9: PL 38, 258), it is as if he were recounting his own life experience. Intellect and faith are not foreign or antagonistic to the divine Revelation but are both conditions for understanding its meaning, for receiving its authentic message, for approaching the threshold of the mystery. Saint Augustine, together with so many other Christian authors, is a witness of a faith that is practiced with reason, that thinks and invites thought. On this same track, Saint Anselm was to say in his *Proslogion* that the Catholic faith is a *fides quaerens intellectum*, where the quest for understanding is an act inherent to believing. It was to be Saint Thomas Aquinas in particular—strong in this tradition—who challenged the reason of the philosophers, showing how much new and fertile rational vitality comes from human thought grafted on to the principles and truths of the Christian faith.

The Catholic faith is therefore reasonable and fosters trust in human reason as well. The First Vatican Council, in the Dogmatic Constitution *Dei Filius*, said that reason is able to know with certainty that God exists through the creation, whereas the possibility of knowing "easily, with complete certainty and without error" (DS 3005) the truths that concern God in the light of grace belongs to faith alone. The knowledge of faith, moreover, is not in opposition to right reason. Blessed Pope John Paul II, in fact, in his Encyclical *Fides et Ratio*, sums it up in these words: "Human reason is neither annulled nor debased in assenting to the contents of faith, which are in any case attained by way of free and informed choice" (no. 43). In the irresistible desire for truth, only a harmonious relationship between faith and reason is the right road that leads to God and to the person's complete fulfillment.

This doctrine is easily recognizable throughout the New Testament. Saint Paul, in writing to the Christians of Corinth, maintains, as we have heard: "Jews demand signs and Greeks seek wisdom, but we preach Christ crucified, a stumbling block to Jews and folly to Gentiles" (1 Cor 1:22–23). God in fact saved the world, not with an act of power, but through the humiliation of his Only-Begotten Son. Measured in human parameters, the unusual ways of God clash with the demands of Greek wisdom. And yet, the Cross of Christ has a reason of its own which Saint Paul calls: *ho logos tou staurou*: "the word of the cross" (1 Cor 1:18). Here the term *logos* means both the word and reason, and, if it alludes to the word, it is because it expresses verbally what reason works out. Hence Paul sees the Cross, not as an irrational event, but as a saving factor that possesses its own reasonableness, recognizable in the light of faith. At the same time, he has such trust in human reason that he is surprised that many people, in spite of seeing the works brought about by God, persist in refusing to believe in him. In his Letter to the Romans, Saint Paul says: "Ever since the creation of the world his invisible nature, namely, his eternal power and deity, has been clearly perceived in the things that have been made" (1:20). Saint Peter likewise also urges the Christians of the diaspora to worship: "In your hearts reverence Christ as Lord. Always be prepared to make a defense to any one who calls you to account for the hope that is in you" (1 Pt 3:15). In an atmosphere of persecution and with a pressing need to bear witness to faith, we believers are asked to justify with well-grounded reasons our adherence to the word of the Gospel, to account for the reason for our hope.

The virtual relationship between science and faith is also founded on these premises concerning the fertile connection between understanding and believing. Scientific research leads to the knowledge of ever new truths about man and about the cosmos, as we see it. The true good of mankind, accessible in faith, unfolds the horizons within which the process of its discovery must move. Consequently, research, for example, at the service of life and which aims to eliminate disease should be encouraged. Also important are investigations that aim to discover the secrets of our planet and of the universe, in the awareness that man is not in charge of creation to exploit it foolishly but to preserve it and make it inhabitable. Thus faith, lived truly, does not come into conflict with science but, rather, cooperates with it, offering the basic criteria to promote the good of all and asking it to give up only those endeavors which—in opposition to God's original plan—produce effects that are detrimental to man. For this reason, too, it is reasonable to believe: if science is a precious ally of faith for understanding God's plan for the universe, faith, remaining faithful to this very plan, permits scientific progress always to be achieved for the good and truth of man.

This is why it is crucial for man to be open to faith and to know God and his plan of salvation in Jesus Christ.

In the Gospel, a new humanism is inaugurated, an authentic "grammar" of man and of the whole of reality. The *Catechism of the Catholic Church* states: "God's truth is his wisdom, which commands the whole created order and governs the world. God, who alone made heaven and earth (cf. Ps 115:15; Wis 7:17–21), can alone impart true knowledge of every created thing in relation to himself" (no. 216).

Let us trust, therefore, that our commitment to evangelization may help to restore a new centrality to the Gospel in the life of untold men and women of our time. And let us pray that all may rediscover in Christ the meaning of existence and the foundation of true freedom: without God, in fact, man loses himself. The testimonies of those who have preceded us and dedicated their lives to the Gospel confirm this forever. It is reasonable to believe, and the whole of our existence is at stake. It is worth expending oneself for Christ; he alone satisfies the desires for truth and goodness that are rooted in every man's soul: now, in time that passes, and in the never-ending day of blessed Eternity.

7

How to Speak about God

WEDNESDAY, 28 NOVEMBER 2012
Paul VI Audience Hall

Dear Brothers and Sisters,

The important question we ask ourselves today is: How can we talk about God in our time? How can we communicate the Gospel so as to open roads to his saving truth in our contemporaries' hearts—which are all too often closed—and minds—which are at times distracted by the many dazzling lights of society? Jesus, the Evangelists tell us, asked himself about this as he proclaimed the Kingdom of God: "With what can we compare the Kingdom of God, or what parable shall we use for it?" (Mk 4:30). How can we talk about God today? The first answer is that we can talk about God because he has talked to us; so the first condition for speaking of God is listening to all that God himself has said. God has spoken to us! God is therefore not a distant hypothesis concerning the world's origin; he is not a mathematical intelligence far from us. God takes an interest in us, he loves us, he has entered personally into the reality of our history, he has communicated himself, even to the point of taking flesh. Thus God is a reality of our life, he is so great that he has time for us, too, he takes an interest in us. In Jesus of Nazareth, we encounter the face of God, who came down from his Heaven to immerse himself in the human world, in our world, and to teach "the art of living", the road to happiness; to set us free from sin and make us children of God (cf. Eph 1:5; Rom 8:14). Jesus came to save us and to show us the good life of the Gospel.

Talking about God means first of all expressing clearly what God we must bring to the men and women of our time: not an abstract God, a hypothesis, but a real God, a God who exists, who has entered history and is present in history; the God of Jesus Christ as an answer to the fundamental question of the meaning of life and of how we should live. Consequently, speaking of God demands familiarity with Jesus and his Gospel; it implies that we have a real, personal knowledge of God and a strong passion for his plan of salvation, without succumbing to the temptation of success, but following God's own method. God's method is that of humility—God makes himself one of us—his method is brought about through the Incarnation in the simple house of Nazareth; through the Grotto of Bethlehem; through the Parable of the Mustard Seed. We must not fear the humility of taking little steps, but trust in the leaven that penetrates the dough and slowly causes it to rise (cf. Mt 13:33). In talking about God, in the work of evangelization, under the guidance of the Holy Spirit, we must recover simplicity, we must return to the essence of the proclamation: the Good News of a God who is real and effective, a God who is concerned about us, a God-Love who makes himself close to us in Jesus Christ, until the Cross, and who in the Resurrection gives us hope and opens us to a life that has no end, eternal life, true life. Saint Paul, that exceptional communicator, gives us a lesson that goes straight to the heart of the problem of faith: "how to speak of God" with great simplicity. In his First Letter to the

Corinthians, he writes: "When I came to you, brethren, I
did not come proclaiming to you the testimony of God in
lofty words or wisdom. For I decided to know nothing
among you except Jesus Christ and him crucified" (2:1–2).
The first real fact, therefore, is that Paul speaks, not of a
philosophy that he developed, not of ideas that he found
elsewhere or invented, but of a reality of his life; he speaks
of the God who entered his life; he speaks of a real God,
who is alive, who spoke with him and will speak with us,
he speaks of the Crucified and Risen Christ. The second
real fact is that Paul does not seek himself, he does not
want to make a fan club for himself, he does not wish to
go down in history as the head of a school of great knowledge, he is not self-seeking; rather, Saint Paul proclaims Christ
and wants to gain people for the true and real God. Paul's
wish is to speak of and preach the One who entered his life
and who is true life, who won him over on the road to
Damascus. Therefore, talking about God means making room
for the One who enables us to know him, who reveals his
face of love to us; it means emptying ourselves of our own
ego, offering it to Christ, in the awareness that it is not we
who can win over others for God, but that we must expect
God to send them, we must entreat God for them. Talking
about God, therefore, stems from listening, from our knowledge of God, which is brought about through familiarity
with him, through the life of prayer and in accordance with
the Commandments.

Communicating faith, for Saint Paul, did not mean putting himself forward but, rather, saying openly and pub-
licly what he had seen and heard in his encounter with
Christ, what he had experienced in his life that was transformed by that encounter: it meant putting forward Jesus,
whom he felt present within him and who became the

true orientation of his existence, to make it clear to all that Jesus is necessary to the world and crucial to every person's freedom. The Apostle is not satisfied with proclaiming words but expends his whole life in the great work of faith. To speak of God, we must leave him room, trusting that he will act in our weakness: we must make room for him without fear but with simplicity and joy, in the deep conviction that the more we put him at the center rather than ourselves, the more fruitful our communication will be. And this is also true for Christian communities: they are called to show the transforming action of God's grace, by overcoming individualism, closure, selfishness, indifference, by living out God's love in their daily relations. Let us ask ourselves whether our communities really are like this. To be so, we must always and truly proclaim Christ and not ourselves.

At this point we should ask ourselves: How did Jesus communicate? Jesus, in his oneness, speaks of his Father—*Abba*—and of the Kingdom of God, his gaze full of compassion for the hardships and difficulties of human life. He speaks with great realism, and I would say that the essential feature of Jesus' proclamation is that it makes clear that our life and the world are worthy of God. Jesus shows that in the world and in creation God's face shines out, and he shows us that God is present in the daily events of our life. Both in the parables on nature, the mustard seed and the field with various seeds, and in our own life—let us think of the Parable of the Prodigal Son, of Lazarus, and of other parables of Jesus. From the Gospels we see that Jesus takes an interest in every human situation that he encounters, he immerses himself in the reality of the men and women of his time, with complete trust in the Father's help. And that in this history, although hidden, God is really present, and if we are attentive we can encounter him. And the disciples, who live with Jesus, and the crowds who meet him see his reaction to the most disparate problems, they see how he speaks, how he behaves; in him they see the action of the Holy Spirit, the action of God. In him proclamation and life are interwoven: Jesus acts and teaches, always starting from a close relationship with God the Father. This style becomes an essential indication for us as Christians: our way of living in faith and charity becomes a way of speaking of God today, because it shows, through a life lived in Christ, the credibility and realism of what we say with words, which are not solely words but reveal the reality, the true reality. And in this we must take care to perceive the signs of the times in our epoch, namely, to identify the potentials, aspirations, and obstacles we encounter in today's culture and in particular the wish for authenticity, the yearning for transcendence, and the concern to safeguard creation, and we must communicate fearlessly the response that faith in God offers. The Year of Faith is an opportunity for us to discover, our imaginations fired by the Holy Spirit, new paths to take on a personal and community level so that the power of the Gospel may become wisdom of life and an orientation for existence everywhere.

In our time, too, the family, the first school for communicating the faith to the new generations, is a privileged place in which to talk about God. The Second Vatican Council speaks of parents as the first messengers of God (cf. Dogmatic Constitution, Decree *Lumen Gentium*, no. 11; *Apostolicam Actuositatem*, no. 11). Parents are called to rediscover their mission, assuming responsibility in educating, in opening the consciences of their little ones to love of God as a fundamental service to their life and in being the first catechists and teachers of the faith for their children. And in this task *watchfulness* is of the utmost importance. It means being able to take favorable opportunities to introduce the topic of faith in the family and to develop a critical reflection with regard to the many forms of conditioning to which children are subjected. The parents' attention includes their sensitivity in perceiving the possible religious questions latent in their children's minds, at times obvious but at other times hidden. Then, *joy*: the communication of faith must always have joyful tones. It is the Easter joy that does not stay silent or conceal the realities of pain, of suffering, of effort, of difficulty, of incomprehension, and of death itself, but that can offer criteria for interpreting all things in the perspective of Christian hope. The good life of the Gospel is precisely this new perception, this capacity to see God with one's own eyes in every situation. It is important to help all the members of the family understand that faith is not a burden but a source of profound joy, that it is perceiving God's action, recognizing the presence of goodness that does not make a sound; and it offers precious guidance for living life well. Lastly, the *capacity for listening and for dialogue*: the family must be a milieu in which we learn to be together, to settle disagreements in conversation with each other, which consists in listening and speaking, in mutual understanding and love, so as to be a sign for each other of God's merciful love.

So it is that talking about God means making people realize through our speech and example that God is no rival in our existence but rather is its true guarantor, who guarantees the greatness of man. Thus we return to the beginning: speaking of God is communicating what is essential, forcefully and simply, through our words and through our life: the God of Jesus Christ, that God who showed us a love so great that he took flesh, died, and rose again for us:

that God who asks us to follow him and to let ourselves be transformed by his immense love in order to renew our life and our relationships; that God who has given us the Church, so that we may walk together and, through the Word and the sacraments, renew the entire city of man so that it may become a City of God.

God Reveals His "Benevolent Purpose"

WEDNESDAY, 5 DECEMBER 2012
Paul VI Audience Hall

Dear Brothers and Sisters,

At the beginning of his Letter to the Christians of Ephesus (cf. 1:3–14), the Apostle Paul raised a prayer of blessing to God, Father of our Lord Jesus Christ, which leads us to experience the Season of Advent in the context of the Year of Faith. The theme of this hymn of praise is God's plan for man, described in terms full of joy, wonder, and thanksgiving, according to his "benevolent purpose" (cf. v. 9) of mercy and love.

Why does the Apostle raise this blessing to God from the depths of his heart? It is because he sees God's action in the perspective of salvation which culminated in the Incarnation, death, and Resurrection of Jesus and contemplates how the heavenly Father chose us even before the world's creation to be his adoptive sons, in his Only-Begotten Son, Jesus Christ (cf. Rom 8:14f.; Gal 4:4f.). We had always existed in God's mind in a great plan that God cherished within himself and decided to implement and to reveal in "the fullness of time" (cf. Eph 1:10). Saint Paul

makes us understand, therefore, how the whole of creation and, in particular, man are not the result of chance
but are part of a benevolent purpose of the eternal reason
of God, who brings the world into being with the creative and redemptive power of his Word. This first affirmation reminds us that our vocation is not merely to exist
in the world, to be inserted into a history, nor is it solely
to be creatures of God. It is something more: it is being
chosen by God, even before the world's creation, in the
Son, Jesus Christ. Therefore in him we have existed, so to
speak, forever. God contemplates us in Christ, as his adoptive sons. God's "purpose", which the Apostle also describes
as a plan "of love" (Eph 1:5), is described as "the mystery" of his divine will (v. 9), hidden and now revealed in
the Person of Christ and in his work. The divine initiative
comes before every human response: it is a freely given
gift of his love that envelops and transforms us.

But what is the ultimate purpose of this mysterious design?
What is the essence of God's will? It is, Saint Paul tells us,
"to unite all things in him [Christ], the Head" (v. 10). In
these words we find one of the central formulas of the New
Testament that makes us understand the plan of God, his
design of love for the whole of mankind, a formula which,
in the second century, Saint Irenaeus of Lyons established
as the core of his Christology: to "recapitulate" the whole
of reality in Christ. Perhaps some of you may remember
the formula used by Pope Saint Pius X for the consecration
of the world to the Sacred Heart of Jesus: "*Instaurare omnia
in Christo*", a formula that refers to the Pauline expression
and was also the motto of this holy Pope. However, the
Apostle speaks more precisely of the recapitulation of the
universe in Christ. This means that in the great plan of
creation and of history, Christ stands as the focus of the

entire journey of the world, as the structural support of all things, and attracts to himself the entire reality in order to overcome dispersion and limitation and lead all things to the fullness desired by God (cf. Eph 1:23).

This "benevolent purpose" was not, so to speak, left in the silence of God, in his heavenly heights. Rather, God made it known by entering into a relationship with man, to whom he did not reveal just something but, indeed, himself. He did not merely communicate an array of truths, but communicated himself to us, even to the point of becoming one of us, of taking flesh. The Second Vatican Ecumenical Council says in the Dogmatic Constitution *Dei Verbum*: "It pleased God, in his goodness and wisdom, to reveal himself [not only something of himself, but himself] and to make known the mystery of his will. His will was that men should have access to the Father, through Christ, the Word made flesh, in the Holy Spirit, and thus become sharers in the divine nature" (no. 2). God does not only say something; rather, he communicates himself, draws us into his divine nature so that we may be integrated into it or divinized. God reveals his great plan of love by entering into a relationship with man, by coming so close to him that he makes himself man. The Council continues: "The invisible God, from the fullness of his love, addresses men as his friends (cf. Ex 33:11; Jn 15:14–15), and moves among them (cf. Bar 3:38), in order to invite and receive them into his own company" (*ibid.*). With his own intelligence and abilities alone, man would not have been able to achieve this most enlightening revelation of God's love; it is God who has opened his Heaven and lowered himself in order to guide man in his ineffable love.

Saint Paul writes further to the Christians of Corinth: "'What no eye has seen, nor ear heard, nor the heart

of man conceived, what God has prepared for those who
love him', God has revealed to us through the Spirit. For
the Spirit searches everything, even the depths of God"
(1 Cor 2:9–10). And Saint John Chrysostom, in a famous
passage commenting on the beginning of the Letter to the
Ephesians, with these words asks that the faithful enjoy the
full beauty of this "loving plan" of God revealed in Christ:
"What do you lack yet? You are made immortal, you are
made free, you are made a son, you are made righteous,
you are made a brother, you are made a fellow-heir, you
reign with Christ, you are glorified with Christ; all things
are freely given you, and, as it is written, 'will he not also
give us all things with him?' (Rom 8:32). Your First-fruits
(cf. 1 Cor 15:20, 23) is adored by Angels. . . . What do you
lack yet?" (PG 62, 11).

This communion in Christ through the action of the
Holy Spirit, offered by God to all men with the light of
Revelation, is not something that is superimposed on our
humanity; it is the fulfillment of our deepest aspirations,
of that longing for the infinite and for fullness, which dwells
in the depths of man and opens him to a happiness that is
not fleeting or limited but eternal. Referring to God who
reveals himself and speaks to us through the Scriptures to
lead us to him, Saint Bonaventure of Bagnoregio says: "Holy
Scripture . . . its words are words of eternal life, and it is
written not just so that we should believe, but specially so
that we should possess eternal life in which we may see,
and love, and have all our desires fulfilled" (*Breviloquium*,
Prologue; *Opera Omnia* V, 201f.). Lastly, Blessed Pope John
Paul II recalled that "Revelation has set within history a
point of reference which cannot be ignored if the mystery
of human life is to be known. Yet this knowledge refers
back constantly to the mystery of God which the human

mind cannot exhaust but can only receive and embrace in faith" (Encyclical *Fides et Ratio*, no. 14).

Therefore, in this perspective, what is the act of faith? It is man's answer to God's Revelation that is made known and expresses his plan of love; to use an Augustinian expression, it is letting oneself be grasped by the Truth that is God, a Truth that is Love. Saint Paul stresses that, since God has revealed his mystery, we owe him "the obedience of faith" (Rom 16:26; cf. 1:5; 2 Cor 10:5–6), by which attitude "man freely commits his entire self to God, making 'the full submission of his intellect and will to God who reveals' and willingly assenting to the Revelation given by him" (Dogmatic Constitution, *Dei Verbum*, no. 5). All this leads to a fundamental change in the way of relating to reality as a whole; everything appears in a new light, so it is a true "conversion"; faith is a "change of mentality". This is because God revealed himself in Christ and made his plan of love known; he takes hold of us, he draws us to him, he becomes the meaning that sustains life, the rock on which to find stability. In the Old Testament, we find a concentrated saying on faith which God entrusted to the Prophet Isaiah so that he might communicate it to Ahaz, King of Judah. God says, "If you will not believe"— that is, if you are not faithful to God—"surely you shall not be established" (Is 7:9b). Thus there is a connection between *being* and *understanding* which clearly expresses that faith is welcoming in life God's view of reality, it is letting God guide us with his words and sacraments in understanding what we should do, what journey we should make, how we should live. Yet at the same time it is, precisely, understanding according to God and seeing with his eyes that makes life sure, that enables us to "stand" rather than fall.

Dear friends, Advent, the liturgical Season that we have just begun and that prepares us for Holy Christmas, sets us before the luminous mystery of the coming of the Son of God, the great "benevolent purpose" with which he wishes to draw us to him, to enable us to live in full communion of joy and peace with him. Advent invites us once again, in the midst of so many difficulties, to renew the certainty that God is present: he entered the world, making himself man, a man like us, to fulfill his plan of love. And God asks that we, too, become a sign of his action in the world. Through our faith, our hope, and our charity, he wants to enter the world ever anew and wants ever anew to make his light shine out in our dark night.

9

The Stages of the Revelation

Dear Brothers and Sisters,

In our Catechesis last week I spoke of the Revelation of God as a communication he makes of himself and of his benevolent and loving purpose. This Revelation of God fits into human time and history: a history that becomes "the arena where we see what God does for humanity. God comes to us in the things we know best and can verify most easily, the things of our everyday routine, apart from which we cannot understand ourselves" (cf. John Paul II, Encyclical *Fides et Ratio*, no. 12).

Saint Mark the Evangelist—as we have heard—records the very start of Jesus' preaching in clear and concise words: "The time is fulfilled, and the kingdom of God is at hand" (Mk 1:15). What illuminates and gives full meaning to the history of the world and of man begins to shine out in the Bethlehem Grotto; it is the Mystery which, in a little while, we shall be contemplating at Christmas: salvation, brought about in Jesus Christ. In Jesus of Nazareth, God shows his face and asks man to choose to recognize and follow him. God's Revelation of himself in history in order to enter into a relationship of loving dialogue with man gives new meaning to the whole human journey. History is not a mere succession of centuries, years, or days, but the time span of a presence that gives full meaning and opens it to sound hope.

Where can we read the stages of this Revelation of God? Sacred Scripture is the best place for discovering the steps of this process, and I would like—once again—to invite everyone, in this Year of Faith, to open the Bible more often, to hold, read, and meditate on it and to pay greater attention to the Readings of Sunday Mass; all this is precious nourishment for our faith.

In reading the Old Testament, we can see how God intervenes in the history of the chosen people, the people with whom he made a covenant: these are not fleeting events that fade into oblivion. Rather, they become a "memory"; taken together they constitute the "history of salvation", kept alive in the consciousness of the People of Israel through the celebration of the salvific events. Thus, in the Book of Exodus, the Lord instructs Moses to celebrate the Jewish Passover, the great event of the liberation from slavery in Egypt, with these words: "This day shall be for you a memorial day, and you shall keep it as a feast to the Lord; throughout your generations you shall observe it as an ordinance for ever" (12:14). Commemorating what God has brought about becomes a sort of constant imperative for the whole People of Israel, so that the passing of time may be marked by the living memory of past events which, in this way, day after day, form history and live on. In the Book of Deuteronomy, Moses addresses the people saying: "Only take heed, and keep your soul diligently, lest you forget the things which your eyes have seen, and lest they depart from your heart all the days of your life; make them known to your children and your children's children" (4:9). Consequently, he also tells us: "Be careful not to forget the things that God has done for us." Faith is nourished by the discovery and memory of the ever faithful God who guides history and constitutes the sound and permanent foundation on which to build our life. The Canticle of the *Magnificat*, which the Virgin Mary addresses to God, is a lofty example of this history of salvation, of this memory that makes and keeps God's action present. Mary exalts God's merciful action in the actual journey of his people, his fidelity to the promises of the covenant that he made to Abraham and his descendants; and all this is a living memory of the divine presence that is never absent (cf. Lk 1:46–55).

For Israel, the Exodus is the central historical event in which God reveals his powerful action. God sets the Israelites free from slavery in Egypt so that they may return to the Promised Land and worship him as the one true Lord. Israel does not set out to be a people like others—so that it might have national independence—but also in order to serve God in worship and in life, to create a place for God where man is obedient to him, where God is present and worshipped in the world—and, of course, not only among the Israelites, but in order to witness to him also among the other peoples. The celebration of this event is to make him present here and now, so that God's action may not be lacking. He fulfilled his plan of liberation and continues to pursue it so that man may recognize and serve his Lord and respond to his action with faith and love.

So it was that God revealed himself not only in the primordial act of the creation, but also by entering our history, the history of a small people which was neither the largest nor the strongest. And this self-revelation of God, which develops through history, culminates in Jesus Christ: God, the *Logos*, the creative Word who is the origin of the world, took on flesh in Jesus and in him showed the true face of God. In Jesus every promise is fulfilled, the history of God with mankind culminates in him. When we read the account of the two disciples on their way to Emmaus which Saint Luke has written down for us, we become clearly aware of the fact that the Person of Christ illuminates the Old Testament, the whole history of salvation, and shows the great unitive design of the two Testaments; it shows the path to his oneness. Jesus, in fact, explains to the two bewildered and disappointed wayfarers that he is the fulfillment of every promise: "And beginning with Moses and all the prophets, he interpreted to them in all the scriptures the things concerning himself" (24:27). The Evangelist records the exclamation of the two disciples after they recognized that their traveling companion was the Lord: "Did not our hearts burn within us while he talked to us on the road, while he opened to us the scriptures?" (v. 32).

The *Catechism of the Catholic Church* summarizes the development of divine Revelation (cf. nos. 54–64): From the very first, the Lord invited man to intimate communion with himself, and, even when through disobedience he lost his friendship, God did not abandon him to the power of death but time and again offered men covenants (cf. *Roman Missal*, Eucharistic Prayer IV). The *Catechism* retraces God's journey with man from the Covenant with Noah after the flood to the call to Abraham to leave his land to be made the father of a multitude of peoples. God forms his People Israel in the event of the Exodus, in the Covenant of Sinai, and in the gift, through Moses, of the Law, in order to be recognized and served as the one living and true God. With the Prophets, God forms his People in the hope of salvation. We know—through Isaiah—of the "second Exodus", the return of the People from the Babylonian Captivity to

their own land, its refoundation; at the same time, however, many were dispersed, and in this way began the uni-
versality of this faith. In the end, not only a king, David, a
son of David, was awaited, but a "Son of man", the salvation of all peoples. Encounters between cultures took place,
first with Babylon and Syria, then also with the Greek multitude. Thus we see how God's path broadens, how it unfolds
increasingly toward the Mystery of Christ, King of the Universe. In Christ, the Revelation in its fullness, God's benevolent purpose, is brought about at last: he makes himself
one of us.

I have reflected on remembering God's action in human
history to show the stages of this great plan of love, wit-
nessed in the Old and New Testaments. It is a single plan
of salvation, addressed to the whole of mankind, gradually
revealed and realized through the power of God, in which
God always reacts to man's responses and finds the new
beginnings of a covenant when man strays. This is fundamental in the journey of faith. We are in the liturgical Season of Advent, which prepares us for Holy Christmas. As
we all know, "advent" means "coming", "presence", and
in ancient times it meant, precisely, the arrival of the king
or emperor in a specific province. For Christians, the word
means a marvelous and overwhelming reality: God himself
has crossed the threshold of his Heaven and has lowered
himself to man; he has made a covenant with him, entering the history of a people; he is a king who came down to
this poor province which is the earth and made a gift to us
of his visit, taking our flesh and becoming a man like us.
Advent invites us to retrace the journey of this presence
and reminds us over and over again that God did not take
himself away from the world, he is not absent, he has not
left us to ourselves, but comes to meet our needs in various

ways that we must learn to discern. And we, too, with our faith, our hope, and our charity, are called every day to perceive this presence and to witness to it in the world, which is often superficial and distracted, and to make the light that illuminated the Grotto of Bethlehem shine out.

10

The Virgin Mary: Icon of Obedient Faith

WEDNESDAY, 19 DECEMBER 2012
Paul VI Audience Hall

Dear Brothers and Sisters,

The Virgin Mary has a special place in the journey of Advent as the One who, in a unique way, awaited the fulfillment of God's promises, welcoming Jesus the Son of God in faith and in the flesh and with full obedience to the divine will. Today, I wish to ponder briefly with you on Mary's faith, starting from the great mystery of the Annunciation.

"*Chaîre kecharitomene, ho Kyrios meta sou*", "Hail, [rejoice] full of grace, the Lord is with you" (Lk 1:28). These are the words—recorded by Luke the Evangelist—with which the Archangel Gabriel addresses Mary. At first sight, the term *chaîre*, "rejoice", seems an ordinary greeting, typical in the Greek world, but if this word is interpreted against the background of the biblical tradition, it acquires a far deeper meaning. The same term occurs four times in the Greek version of the Old Testament and always as a proclamation of joy in the coming of the Messiah (cf. Zeph 3:14; Joel 2:21; Zech 9:9; Lam 4:21). The Angel's greeting to Mary is therefore an invitation to joy, deep joy. It announces an end to the sadness that exists in the world because of life's limitations, suffering, death, wickedness, in all that seems to block out the light of the divine goodness. It is a greeting that marks the beginning of the Gospel, the Good News.

But why is Mary invited to rejoice in this way? The answer is to be found in the second part of the greeting: "The Lord is with you." Here, too, if we are to understand correctly the meaning of these words, we must turn to the Old Testament. In the Book of Zephaniah, we find these words: "Sing aloud, O daughter of Zion.... The King of Israel, the Lord, is in your midst.... The Lord, your God, is in your midst, a warrior who gives victory" (3:14–17). In these words a twofold promise is made to Israel, to the daughter of Zion: God will come as a savior and will pitch his tent in his people's midst, in the womb of the daughter of Zion. This promise is fulfilled to the letter in the dialogue between the Angel and Mary. Mary is identified with the people espoused by God, she is truly the daughter of Zion in person; in her the expectation of the definitive coming of God is fulfilled, in her the Living God makes his dwelling place.

In the greeting of the Angel, Mary is called "full of grace". In Greek, the term "grace", *charis*, has the same linguistic root as the word "joy". In this term, too, the source of Mary's exultation is further clarified: her joy comes from grace, that is, from being in communion with God, from having such a vital connection with him, from being the dwelling place of the Holy Spirit, totally fashioned by God's action. Mary is the creature who opened the door to her Creator in a special way, placing herself in his hands without reserve. She lived entirely *from* and *in* her relationship with the Lord; she was disposed to listen, alert to recognizing the signs of God in the journey of his people; she was integrated into a history of faith and hope in God's promises with which the fabric of her life was woven. And she submitted freely to the word received, to the divine will in the obedience of faith.

The Evangelist Luke tells Mary's story by aligning it closely to the history of Abraham. Just as the great Patriarch is the father of believers who responded to God's call to leave the land in which he lived, to leave behind all that guaranteed his security in order to start out on the journey to an unknown land, assured only in the divine promise, so Mary trusts implicitly in the word that the messenger of God has announced to her and becomes the model and Mother of all believers.

I would like to emphasize another important point: the opening of the soul to God and to his action in faith also includes an element of obscurity. The relationship of the human being with God does not delete the distance between Creator and creature, it does not eliminate what the Apostle Paul said before the depth of God's wisdom: "How unsearchable are his judgments and how inscrutable his ways!" (Rom 11:33). Yet those who—like Mary—open themselves totally to God come to accept the divine will, even though it is mysterious, even though it often does not correspond with their own wishes and is a sword that pierces their soul, as the elderly Simeon would say prophetically to Mary when Jesus was presented in the Temple (cf. Lk 2:35). Abraham's journey of faith included the moment of joy in the gift of his son Isaac, but also the period of darkness, when he had to climb Mount Moriah to execute a paradoxical order: God was asking him to sacrifice the son he had just given him. On the mountain, the Angel told him: "Do not lay your hand on the lad or do anything to him; for now I know that you fear God, seeing you have not withheld your son, your only son, from me" (Gen 22:12). Abraham's full trust in the God who is faithful to his promises did not fail, even when his word was mysterious and difficult, almost impossible to accept. So it is with Mary. Her faith experienced the joy of the Annunciation, but also passed through the gloom of the crucifixion of the Son to be able to reach the light of the Resurrection.

It is exactly the same on the journey of faith of each one of us: we encounter patches of light, but we also encounter stretches in which God seems absent, when his silence weighs on our hearts and his will does not correspond with ours, with our inclination to do as we like. However, the more we open ourselves to God, welcome the gift of faith, and put our whole trust in him—like Abraham, like Mary—the more capable he will make us, with his presence, of living every situation of life in peace and assured of his faithfulness and his love. However, this means coming out of ourselves and our own projects so that the Word of God may be the lamp that guides our thoughts and actions.

I would like once again to ponder on an aspect that surfaces in the infancy narratives of Jesus recounted by Saint Luke. Mary and Joseph take their Son to Jerusalem, to the Temple, to present him to the Lord and to consecrate him as required by Mosaic Law: "Every firstborn male shall be designated as holy to the Lord" (cf. Lk 2:22–24). The Holy Family's action acquires an even more profound meaning if we interpret it in the light of the evangelical knowledge of the twelve-year-old Jesus. After three days of searching, he was found in the Temple in conversation with the teachers. The deeply anxious words of Mary and Joseph: "Son, why have you treated us so? Behold, your father and I have been looking for you anxiously", are in conformity with Jesus' mysterious answer: "How is it that you sought me?

Did you not know that I must be in my Father's house?"
(Lk 2:48–49). Which is to say, in the Father's property, "in
my Father's house", as a son is. Mary is obliged to renew
the profound faith with which she said "yes" at the Annunciation; she must accept that it is the true and proper Father
of Jesus who has precedence; she must be able to leave the
Son she has brought forth free to follow his mission. And
Mary's "yes" to God's will, in the obedience of faith, is
repeated throughout her life, until the most difficult moment,
that of the Cross.

   Confronting all this, we may ask ourselves: How was Mary
able to journey on beside her Son with such a strong faith,
even in darkness, without losing her full trust in the action
of God? Mary assumes a fundamental approach in facing
what happens in her life. At the Annunciation, on hearing
the Angel's words, she is distressed—it is the fear a person
feels when moved by God's closeness—but it is not the attitude of someone who is afraid of what God might ask.
Mary reflects, she ponders on the meaning of this greeting
(cf. Lk 1:29). The Greek word used in the Gospel to define
this "reflection", "*dielogizeto*", calls to mind the etymology
of the word "dialogue". This means that Mary enters into
a deep conversation with the Word of God that has been
announced to her; she does not consider it superficially but
meditates on it, lets it sink into her mind and her heart so
as to understand what the Lord wants of her, the meaning
of the announcement. We find another hint of Mary's inner
attitude to God's action—again in the Gospel according to
Saint Luke—at the time of Jesus' birth, after the adoration
of the shepherds. Luke affirms that Mary "kept all these
things, pondering them in her heart" (Lk 2:19). In Greek,
the term is *symballon*; we could say that she "kept together",
"pieced together" in her heart all the events that were

happening to her; she placed every individual element, every word, every event, within the whole and confronted it, cherished it, recognizing that it all came from the will of God. Mary does not stop at a first superficial understanding of what is happening in her life but, rather, can look in depth; she lets herself be called into question by events, digests them, discerns them, and attains the understanding that only faith can provide. It is the profound humility of the obedient faith of Mary, who welcomes within her even what she does not understand in God's action, leaving it to God to open her mind and heart. "Blessed is she who believed that there would be a fulfillment of what was spoken to her from the Lord" (Lk 1:45), her kinswoman Elizabeth exclaims. It is exactly because of this faith that all generations will call her blessed.

Dear friends, the Solemnity of the Nativity of the Lord which we shall soon be celebrating invites us to practice this same humility and obedience of faith. The glory of God is not expressed in the triumph and power of a king, it does not shine out in a famous city or a sumptuous palace but makes its abode in a virgin's womb and is revealed in the poverty of a child. In our lives, too, the almightiness of God acts with the force—often in silence—of truth and love. Thus faith tells us that, in the end, the defenseless power of that Child triumphs over the clamor of worldly powers.

11

He Was Conceived by the Holy Spirit

WEDNESDAY, 2 JANUARY 2013
Paul VI Audience Hall

Dear Brothers and Sisters,

Once again the Nativity of the Lord illuminates the gloom that often envelops our world and our hearts and with its light brings hope and joy. Where does this light come from? From the Bethlehem Grotto where the shepherds found "Mary and Joseph, and the babe, lying in a manger" (Lk 2:16). Another, deeper question arises before this Holy Family: How can that tiny, frail Child have brought into the world a newness so radical that it changed the course of history? Is there not perhaps something mysterious about his origins which goes beyond that grotto?

The question of Jesus' origins recurs over and over again. It is the same question that the Procurator Pontius Pilate asked during the trial: "Where are you from?" (Jn 19:9). Yet his origins were quite clear. In John's Gospel when the Lord says: "I am the bread which came down from heaven", the Jews reacted, murmuring: "Is not this Jesus, the son of Joseph, whose father and mother we know? How does he now say, 'I have come down from heaven'?" (Jn 6:41, 42). Moreover, a little later the citizens of Jerusalem strongly opposed Jesus' messianic claim, asserting that "where this

67

man comes from" was well known and that "when the Christ appears, no one will know where he comes from" (Jn 7:27). Jesus himself points out how inadequate their claim to know his origins is, and by so doing he already offers a clue to knowing where he came from: "I have not come of my own accord; he who sent me is true, and him you do not know" (Jn 7:28). Jesus was of course a native of Nazareth, he was born in Bethlehem; but what is known of his true origins?

In the four Gospels, the answer is clear as to where Jesus "comes from". His true origins are in the Father, God; he comes totally from him [God], but in a different way from that of any of God's Prophets or messengers who preceded him. This origin in the mystery of God, "whom no one knows" is already contained in the infancy narratives in the Gospels of Matthew and Luke that we are reading during this Christmastide. The Angel Gabriel proclaimed: "The Holy Spirit will come upon you, and the power of the Most High will overshadow you; therefore the child to be born will be called holy, the Son of God" (Lk 1:35). We repeat these words every time we recite the *Creed*, the Profession of Faith: "*Et incarnatus est de Spiritu Sancto, ex Maria Virgine*", "and by the Holy Spirit was incarnate of the Virgin Mary". At this sentence we kneel, for the veil that concealed God is lifted, as it were, and his unfathomable and inaccessible mystery touches us: God becomes the Emmanuel, "God-with-us". When we hear the Masses written by the great composers of sacred music—I am thinking, for example, of Mozart's Coronation Mass—we immediately notice how they pause on this phrase in a special way, as if they were trying to express in the universal language of music what words cannot convey: the great mystery of God who took flesh, who was made man.

If we consider carefully the words: "by the Holy Spirit [he] was incarnate of the Virgin Mary", we notice that they include four active subjects. The Holy Spirit and Mary are mentioned explicitly, but "he", namely, the Son, who took flesh in the Virgin's womb, is implicit. In the Profession of Faith, the *Creed*, Jesus is described with several epithets: "Lord ... Christ, Only-Begotten Son of God ... God from God, Light from Light, true God from true God ... consubstantial with the Father" (*Niceno-Constantinopolitan Creed*). We can therefore see that "he" refers to another person, the Father. Consequently, the first subject of this sentence is the Father who, with the Son and the Holy Spirit, is the one God.

This affirmation of the *Creed* does not concern God's eternal being but, rather, speaks to us of an action in which the three divine Persons take part and which is brought about "*ex Maria Virgine*". Without Mary, God's entry into the history of mankind would not have achieved its purpose, and what is central to our Profession of Faith would not have taken place: God is a "God-with-us". Thus Mary belongs irrevocably to our faith in God who acts, who enters history. She makes her whole person available, she "agrees" to become God's dwelling place.

Sometimes, on our journey and in our life of faith, we can sense our poverty, our inadequacy in the face of the witness we must offer to the world. However, God chose, precisely, a humble woman, in an unknown village, in one of the most distant provinces of the great Roman Empire. We must always trust in God, even in the face of the most grueling difficulties, renewing our faith in his presence and action in our history, just as in Mary's. Nothing is impossible to God! With him our existence always journeys on safe ground and is open to a future of firm hope.

In professing in the *Creed*: "by the Holy Spirit was incarnate of the Virgin Mary", we affirm that the Holy Spirit, as the power of the Most High God, mysteriously brought about in the Virgin Mary the conception of the Son of God. The Evangelist Luke recorded the Archangel Gabriel's words: "The Holy Spirit will come upon you, and the power of the Most High will overshadow you" (1:35). Two references are obvious: the first is to the moment of the creation. At the beginning of the Book of Genesis we read that "the Spirit of God was moving over the face of the waters" (1:2); this is the Creator Spirit who gave life to all things and to man. What is brought about in Mary, through the action of this same divine Spirit, is a new creation: God, who called forth being from nothing, by the Incarnation gives life to a new beginning of mankind. The Fathers of the Church sometimes speak of Christ as the new Adam in order to emphasize that the new creation began with the birth of the Son of God in the Virgin Mary's womb. This makes us think about how faith also brings us a newness so strong that it produces a second birth. Indeed, at the beginning of our life as Christians, there is Baptism, which causes us to be reborn as children of God and makes us share in the filial relationship that Jesus has with the Father. And I would like to point out that Baptism is *received*, we "are baptized"—it is passive—because no one can become a son of God on his own. It is a gift that is freely given. Saint Paul recalls this adoptive sonship of Christians in a central passage of his Letter to the Romans, where he writes: "All who are led by the Spirit of God are sons of God. For you did not receive the spirit of slavery to fall back into fear, but you have received the spirit of sonship. When we cry, 'Abba! Father!' it is the Spirit himself bearing witness with our spirit that we are children of God" (Rom 8:14–16), not slaves. Only if we open ourselves to God's action, like Mary, only if we entrust our life to the Lord as to a friend whom we totally trust, will everything change, will our whole life acquire a new meaning, a new aspect: that of children with a father who loves us and never deserts us.

We have spoken of two elements: the first was the Spirit moving on the surface of the waters, the Creator Spirit: there is another element in the words of the Annunciation. The Angel said to Mary: "The power of the Most High will over-shadow you." This is a re-evocation of the holy cloud that, during the Exodus, halted over the tent of meeting, over the Ark of the Covenant that the People of Israel were carrying with them and that indicated God's presence (cf. Ex 40:34–38). Mary, therefore, is the new holy tent, the new ark of the covenant: with her "yes" to the Archangel's words, God received a dwelling place in this world, the One whom the universe cannot contain took up his abode in a Virgin's womb.

Let us therefore return to the initial question, the one about Jesus' origins that is summed up by Pilate's question: "Where are you from?" What Jesus' true origins are is clear from our reflections, from the very beginning of the Gospels: he is the Only-Begotten Son of the Father, he comes from God. We have before us the great and overwhelming mys-tery which we are celebrating in this Christmas season. The Son of God, through the work of the Holy Spirit, was incar-nate in the womb of the Virgin Mary. This is an announce-ment that rings out ever new and in itself brings hope and joy to our hearts because, every time, it gives us the cer-tainty that even though we often feel weak, poor, and inca-pable in the face of the difficulties and evil in the world, God's power is always active and works miracles through weakness itself. His grace is our strength (cf. 2 Cor 12:9–10).

12

He Became a Man

WEDNESDAY, 9 JANUARY 2013
Paul VI Audience Hall

Dear Brothers and Sisters,

In this Christmas season, let us reflect once again on the great mystery of God who came down from Heaven to enter our flesh. In Jesus, God was incarnate, he became a man like us and in this way opened for us the road to his heavenly Kingdom, to full communion with him.

In these days, the term the "Incarnation" of God has rung out several times in our churches, expressing the reality we celebrate at Holy Christmas: the Son of God was made man, as we say in the *Creed*. But what does this word, so central to the Christian faith, mean? Incarnation derives from the Latin *incarnatio*. Saint Ignatius of Antioch—at the end of the first century—and, especially, Saint Irenaeus used this term in reflecting on the Prologue to the Gospel according to Saint John, in particular in the sentence "the Word became flesh" (Jn 1:14). Here the word "flesh", according to the Hebrew usage, indicates man in his whole self, the whole man, but in particular in the dimension of his transience and his temporality, his poverty and his contingency. This was in order to tell us that the salvation brought by God, who became man in Jesus of Nazareth, affects man in his material reality and in whatever situation he may be. God assumed the human condition to heal it from all that separates it from him, to enable us to call him, in his Only-Begotten Son, by the name of "Abba, Father" and truly to be children of God. Saint Irenaeus stated: "For this is why the Word became man, and the Son of God became the Son of man: so that man, by entering into communion with the Word and thus receiving divine sonship, might become a son of God" (*Adversus Haereses* 3, 19, 1: PG 7, 939; cf. *Catechism of the Catholic Church*, no. 460).

"The Word was made flesh" is one of those truths to which we have grown so accustomed that the greatness of the event it expresses barely makes an impression on us. And, actually, in this Christmastide in which these words often recur in the Liturgy, we at times pay more attention to the external aspects, to the "colors" of the celebration, than to the heart of the great Christian newness that we are celebrating: something that utterly defeats the imagination, that God alone could bring about and into which we can only enter with faith. The *Logos*, who is with God, the *Logos* who is God, the Creator of the world (cf. Jn 1:1) through whom all things were created (cf. 1:3) and who has accompanied man through history with his light (cf. 1:4–5; 1:9), became one among many and made his dwelling among us, becoming one of us (cf. 2:14). The Second Vatican Ecumenical Council said: "The Son of God . . . worked with human hands, he thought with a human mind. He acted with a human will, and with a human heart he loved. Born of the Virgin Mary, he has truly been made one of us, like to us in all things except sin" (Constitution *Gaudium et Spes*, no. 22). Thus it is important to recover our wonder at the mystery, to let ourselves be enveloped by the grandeur of this event: God, the true God, Creator of all, walked our roads as a man, entering human time to communicate his own life to us (cf. 1 Jn 1:1–4). And he did so, not with the splendor of a sovereign who dominates the world with his power, but with the humility of a child.

I would like to stress a second element. At Holy Christmas we generally exchange a few gifts with the people closest to us. At times this may be a conventional gesture, but it usually expresses affection; it is a sign of love and esteem. In the Prayer over the Offerings at the Vigil Mass of the Solemnity of Christmas, the Church prays: "May the oblation of this day's feast be pleasing to you, O Lord, we pray, that through this most holy exchange we may be found in the likeness of Christ in whom our nature is united to you. Who lives and reigns for ever." The idea of giving is, therefore, at the heart of the Liturgy and makes us aware of the original gift of Christmas: on that Holy Night, in taking flesh God wanted to make a gift of himself to men, he gave himself for us; God made his Only Son a gift for us, he took on our humanity to give his divinity to us. This is the great gift. In our giving, too, it does not matter whether or not a gift is expensive; those who cannot manage to give a little of themselves always give too little. Indeed, at times we even seek to substitute money or material things for our hearts and the commitment to give ourselves. The mystery of the Incarnation shows that God did not do this: he did not give some thing but he gave himself in his Only-Begotten Son. We find here our model for giving so that our relationships, especially those that are most important, may be guided by the gratuitiveness of love.

I would like to offer a third thought: the event of the Incarnation, of God who became man, like us, shows us the daring realism of divine love. God's action, in fact, was not limited to words. On the contrary, we might say that he was not content with speaking, but entered into our history, taking upon himself the effort and burden of human life. The Son of God truly became a man. He was born of the Virgin Mary in a specific time and place, in Bethlehem during the reign of the Emperor Augustus, under the Governor Quirinius (cf. Lk 2:1–2); he grew up in a family, he had friends, he formed a group of disciples, he instructed the Apostles to continue his mission, and ended the course of his earthly life on the Cross. The way God acted gives us a strong incentive to question ourselves on the reality of our faith, which must not be limited to the sphere of sentiment, of the emotions; rather, it must enter into the practicality of our existence, that is, it must touch our everyday life and give it practical guidance. God did not stop at words, but showed us how to live, sharing in our own experience, except for sin. The *Catechism of Saint Pius X*, which some of us studied as children, answers with simple brevity the question "What must we do to live according to the will of God?": "To live according to the will of God, we must believe the truths that he has revealed and obey his commandments with the help of his grace, which is obtained through the sacraments and through prayer." Faith has a fundamental aspect that involves not only our mind and heart but also our whole life.

I suggest one last element for you to think about. Saint John says that the Word, the *Logos*, was with God in the beginning and that everything was done through the Word and nothing that exists was done without him (cf. Jn 1:1–13). The Evangelist is clearly alluding to the creation narrative in the first chapters of the Book of Genesis and reinterprets it in the light of Christ. This is a fundamental criterion in the Christian interpretation of the Bible: The Old and New Testaments should always be read together, and, starting with the New, the deepest meaning of the Old Testament is also revealed. That same Word, who has always existed with God, who is God himself and through whom and for whom all things were created (cf. Col 1:16–17), became man: the eternal and infinite God immersed himself in human finiteness, in his creature, to bring back man and the whole of creation to himself. The *Catechism of the Catholic Church* says: "The first creation finds its meaning and its summit in the new creation in Christ, the splendor of which surpasses that of the first creation" (no. 349). The Fathers of the Church compared Jesus to Adam, even to the point of calling him "the second Adam", or the definitive Adam, the perfect image of God. With the Incarnation of the Son of God, a new creation was brought about that gave the complete answer to the question "Who is man?" God's plan for man was fully manifest in Jesus alone. He is the definitive man according to God's will. The Second Vatican Council reasserted this forcefully: "In reality it is only in the mystery of the Word made flesh that the mystery of man truly becomes clear. . . . Christ the new Adam . . . fully reveals man to himself and brings to light his most high calling" (Constitution on the Church in the Modern World, *Gaudium et Spes*, no. 22; cf. *Catechism of the Catholic Church*, no. 359). In that Child, the Son of God contemplated at Christmas, we can recognize the true face not only of God but also of man; and only by opening ourselves to his grace and seeking to follow him every day do we fulfill God's plan for us, for each one of us.

Dear friends, during this period let us meditate on the great and marvelous richness of the Mystery of the Incarnation, to permit the Lord to illuminate us and to change us, more and more, into an image of his Son made man for us.

13

Jesus Christ, "Mediator and Sum Total of Revelation"

WEDNESDAY, 16 JANUARY 2013
Paul VI Audience Hall

Dear Brothers and Sisters,

In the Constitution on Divine Revelation, *Dei Verbum*, the Second Vatican Council states that the intimate truth of the whole Revelation of God shines forth for us "in Christ, who is himself both the mediator and the sum total of Revelation" (no. 2). The Old Testament tells us that after the creation—in spite of original sin, in spite of man's arrogance in wishing to put himself in his Creator's place—God once again offers us the possibility of his friendship, especially through the Covenant with Abraham and the journey of a small people, the People of Israel. He did not choose this people with the criteria of earthly power but simply out of love. It was a choice that remains a mystery and reveals the style of God, who calls some, not in order to exclude the others, but so that they may serve as a bridge that leads to him. A choice is always a choice for the other. In the history of the People of Israel, we can retrace the stages of a long journey during which God made himself known, revealed himself, and entered history with words and actions. In order to do this, he used mediators, such as Moses, the Prophets, and the Judges, who communicated his will to the people, reminding them of the requirement of faithfulness to the Covenant and keeping alive their expectation of the complete and definitive fulfillment of the divine promises.

At Holy Christmas, we contemplated the realization of these very promises: the Revelation of God reaching its culmination, its fullness. In Jesus of Nazareth, God really visited his people, he visited mankind in a manner that surpassed every expectation: he sent his Only-Begotten Son: God himself became man. Jesus does not tell us something about God, he does not merely speak of the Father but is the Revelation of God, because he is God and thus reveals the face of God. In the Prologue to his Gospel, Saint John wrote: "No one has ever seen God; the only Son, who is in the bosom of the Father, he has made him known" (Jn 1:18).

I would like to dwell on the phrase: "reveals God's face". In this regard Saint John, in his Gospel, records for us a significant event, which we have just heard. When he is approaching the Passion, Jesus reassures his disciples, asking them not to be afraid and to have faith; he then begins a conversation with them in which he talks about God the Father (cf. Jn 14:2–9). At a certain point the Apostle Philip asks Jesus: "Lord, show us the Father, and we shall be satisfied" (Jn 14:8). Philip is very practical and prosaic, he even says what we ourselves would like to say: "We want to see him, show us the Father"; he asks to "see" the Father, to see his face. Jesus' answer is a reply not only to Philip but also to us, and it ushers us into the heart of Christological faith; the Lord affirms: "He who has seen me has seen the Father" (Jn 14:9). These words sum up the newness of the

New Testament, that newness which appeared in the Bethlehem Grotto: God can be seen, God has shown his face, he is visible in Jesus Christ.

The theme of the "quest for God's face", the desire to know this face, the desire to see God as he is, is clearly present throughout the Old Testament, to the extent that the Hebrew term *p[-]anîm*, which means "face", recurs four hundred times and refers to God one hundred times. One hundred times it refers to God: to the wish to see God's face. Yet the Jewish religion absolutely forbids images, for God cannot be portrayed as, on the contrary, he was portrayed by the neighboring peoples who worshipped idols; therefore, with this prohibition of images the Old Testament seems totally to exclude any "seeing" from worship and from devotion. Yet what did seeking God's face mean to the devout Israelite, who knew that there could be no depiction of it? The question is important: there was a wish, on the one hand, to say that God cannot be reduced to an object, like an image that can be held in the hand, nor can anything be put in God's place; on the other, it was affirmed that God has a face—meaning he is a "you" who can enter into a relationship—and who has not withdrawn into his heavenly dwelling place, looking down at mankind from on high. God is certainly above all things, but he addresses us, he listens to us, he sees us, he speaks to us, he makes a covenant, he is capable of love. The history of salvation is the history of God with mankind, it is the history of this relationship of God who gradually reveals himself to man, who makes himself, his face, known.

At the very beginning of the year, on 1 January, we heard in the Liturgy the most beautiful prayer of blessing upon the people: "May the Lord bless you and keep you. May the Lord make his face shine on you, and be gracious to you. May the Lord uncover his face to you and bring you peace" (Num 6:24–26). The splendor of the divine face is the source of life; it is what makes it possible to see reality; the light of his face is guidance for life. In the Old Testament, there is a figure with whom the theme of "the face of God" is connected in a special way: Moses. The man whom God chose to set his people free from slavery in Egypt, giving him the Law of the Covenant and leading him to the Promised Land. Well, in Chapter 33 of the Book of Exodus, it says that Moses had a close and confidential relationship with God: "The Lord used to speak to Moses face to face, as a man speaks to his friend" (v. 11). By virtue of this trust, Moses was able to ask God: "Show me your glory", and God's response was clear: "'I will make all my goodness pass before you, and will proclaim before you my name. . . .' 'But,' he said 'you cannot see my face; for man shall not see me and live. . . . There is a place by me. . . . You shall see my back; but my face shall not be seen'" (vv. 18–23). Thus, there was, on the one hand, the face-to-face conversation as between friends but, on the other, the impossibility in this life of seeing the face of God, which remained hidden; sight is restricted. The Fathers said that these words, "you shall see my back", meant you can only follow Christ, and in following him you see the mystery of God from behind; God can be followed by seeing his back.

Something completely new happened, however, with the Incarnation. The search for God's face was given an unimaginable turning point, because this time this face could be seen: it is the face of Jesus, of the Son of God who became man. In him the process of the Revelation of God, which began with Abraham's call, finds fulfillment in the One who is the fullness of this Revelation, because he is the Son of God, he is both "the mediator and the sum total of

Revelation" (Dogmatic Constitution *Dei Verbum*, no. 2), the content of Revelation and the Revealer coincide in him. Jesus shows us God's face and makes God's name known to us. In the Priestly Prayer at the Last Supper, he says to the Father: "I have manifested your name to the men. . . . I made known to them your name" (cf. Jn 17:6; 6, 26). The phrase: "name of God" means God as the One who is present among men. God had revealed his name to Moses by the burning bush, that is, he had made it possible to call on him, had given a tangible sign of his "being" among men. All this found fulfillment and completion in Jesus: he inaugurated God's presence in history in a new way, because whoever sees him sees the Father, as he said to Philip (cf. Jn 14:9). Christianity, Saint Bernard said, is the "religion of God's word"; yet "not a written and mute word, but an incarnate and living Word" (*Homilia Super Missus Est* 4, 11: PL 183, 86b). In the patristic and medieval tradition, a special formula is used to express this reality: it says that Jesus is the *Verbum abbreviatum* (cf. Rom 9:28, with a reference to Is 10:23), the abbreviated Word, the short and essential Word of the Father who has told us all about him. In Jesus the whole Word is present.

In Jesus, too, the mediation between God and man attains fulfillment. In the Old Testament, there is an array of figures who carried out this role, in particular Moses, the deliverer, the guide, the "mediator" of the Covenant, as he is defined in the New Testament (cf. Gal 3:19; Acts 7:35; Jn 1:17). Jesus, true God and true man, is not simply one of the mediators between God and man but, rather, "the mediator" of the new and eternal Covenant (cf. Heb 8:6; 9:15; 12:24); "for there is one God", Paul says, "and there is one *mediator* between God and men, the man Christ Jesus" (1 Tim 2:5 cf. Gal 3:19–20). In him we see and encounter the Father; in him we can call upon God with the name of "Abba, Father"; in him we are given salvation.

The desire to know God truly, that is, to see God's face, is innate in every man, even in atheists. And perhaps we unconsciously have this wish simply to see who he is, what he is, who he is for us. However, this desire is fulfilled in following Christ, in this way we see his back, and, in the end, we see God, too, as a friend; in Christ's face we see his face. The important thing is that we follow Christ not only in our needy moments or when we find time in our daily occupations, but in our life as such. The whole of our life must be oriented to meeting Jesus Christ, to loving him; and in our life we must allocate a central place to loving our neighbor, that love which, in the light of the Crucified One, enables us to recognize the face of Jesus in the poor, in the weak, and in the suffering. This is only possible if the true face of Jesus has become familiar to us through listening to his word, in an inner conversation with him, in entering this word so that we truly meet him, and, of course, in the Mystery of the Eucharist. In the Gospel of Saint Luke, the passage about the two disciples of Emmaus recognizing Jesus in the breaking of bread is important; prepared by the journey with him, by the invitation to stay with them that they had addressed to him, and by the conversation that made their hearts burn within them, in the end they saw Jesus. For us, too, the Eucharist is the great school in which we learn to see God's face, in which we enter into a close relationship with him; and at the same time we learn to turn our gaze to the final moment of history he will satisfy us with the light of his face. On earth when we are walking toward this fullness, in the joyful expectation that the Kingdom of God will really be brought about.

14

"I believe in God"

WEDNESDAY, 23 JANUARY 2013
Paul VI Audience Hall

Dear Brothers and Sisters,

In this Year of Faith, today I would like to begin to reflect with you on the *Creed*, that is, on the solemn profession of faith that accompanies our life as believers. The opening words of the Creed are: "I believe in God". It is a fundamental affirmation, seemingly simple in its essence, but it opens onto the infinite world of the relationship with the Lord and with his mystery. Believing in God entails adherence to him, the acceptance of his word, and joyful obedience to his Revelation. As the *Catechism of the Catholic Church* teaches, "Faith is a personal act—the free response of the human person to the initiative of God who reveals himself" (no. 166). The ability to say one believes in God is therefore both a gift—God reveals himself, he comes to meet us—and a commitment; it is divine grace and human responsibility in an experience of conversation with God, who, out of love, "addresses men as his friends" (*Dei Verbum*, no. 2), speaks to us, so that, in faith and with faith, we are able to enter into communion with him.

Where can we listen to God and to his Word? Sacred Scripture, in which the Word of God becomes audible to

83

us and nourishes our life as "friends" of God, is fundamental. The entire Bible narrates God's Revelation of himself to mankind. The entire Bible speaks of faith and teaches us faith by narrating a history in which God carries out his plan of redemption and makes himself close to people through an array of shining figures who believe in him and entrust themselves to him, to the fullness of Revelation in the Lord Jesus.

Chapter 11 of the Letter to the Hebrews that we have just heard is very beautiful in this regard. Here faith is discussed and light is shed on the great biblical figures who lived it, becoming models for all believers. In the first verse, the text says: "Faith is the assurance of things hoped for, the conviction of things not seen" (11:1). The eyes of faith are thus able to see the invisible, and the believer's heart can hope beyond all hope, exactly like Abraham, of whom Paul says in the Letter to the Romans: "In hope he believed against hope" (4:18).

And it is on Abraham himself that I wish to reflect and to focus our attention, since he is the first great figure and reference for speaking of faith in God: Abraham the great Patriarch, an exemplary model, father of all believers (cf. Rom 4:11–12). The Letter to the Hebrews presents it in this way: "By faith Abraham obeyed when he was called to go out to a place which he was to receive as an inheritance; and he went out, not knowing where he was to go. By faith he sojourned in the land of promise, as in a foreign land, living in tents like Isaac and Jacob had, heirs with him of the same promise. For he looked forward to the city which has sound foundations, whose builder and maker is God" (11:8–10).

The author of the Letter to the Hebrews is referring here to the call of Abraham, recounted in the Book of Genesis,

the first book of the Bible. What did God ask of this Patriarch? He asked him to set out, leave his own country to
journey to the land that he would show him: "Go from
your country and your kindred and your father's house to
the land that I will show you" (Gen 12:1). How would we
have responded to such an invitation? In fact, it meant setting out with no directions, no knowledge of where God
would lead him; it was a journey that demanded radical
obedience and trust, to which faith alone gives access. Yet
the dark unknown—to which Abraham had to go—was lit
by the light of a promise; God added to his order a reassuring word that unfolded to Abraham a future, life in fullness: "I will make of you a great nation, and I will bless
you, and make your name great . . . and by you all the families of the earth shall bless themselves" (Gen 12:2, 3).

In Sacred Scripture, the blessing is primarily linked to
the gift of life that comes from God and is revealed first of
all in fertility, in a life that is multiplied, passing from one
generation to the next. And also linked to the blessing is
the experience of the possession of a land, a permanent
place in which to live and to develop in freedom and safety,
fearing God and building a society of people faithful to
the Covenant, "a kingdom of priests and a holy nation"
(cf. Ex 19:6).

Therefore, in the divine plan, Abraham was destined to
become "the father of a multitude of nations" (Gen 17:5;
cf. Rom 4:17–18) and to enter a new land in which to
dwell. Yet Sarah, his wife, was barren, she was unable to
bear children; and the land to which God was leading him
was far from the land of his birth, it was already inhabited
by other peoples and would never really belong to him.
The biblical narrator emphasizes this, although with great
discretion: when Abraham arrives in the place of God's

promise: "at that time the Canaanites were in the land" (Gen 12:6). The land that God gave Abraham did not belong to him; he was a foreigner and would always remain such, with all that this implies: having no ambition to possess, ever aware of his poverty, seeing everything as a gift. This is also the spiritual condition of those who agree to follow the Lord, who decide to set out in response to his call, under the banner of his invisible but powerful blessing. And Abraham, "father of believers", accepted this call in faith. Saint Paul wrote in the Letter to the Romans: "In hope he believed against hope, that he should become the father of many nations; as he had been told, 'so shall your descendants be.' He did not weaken in faith when he considered his own body, which was as good as dead because he was about a hundred years old, or when he considered the barrenness of Sarah's womb. No distrust made him waver concerning the promise of God, but he grew strong in his faith as he gave glory to God, fully convinced that God was able to do what he had promised" (Rom 4:18–21).

Faith led Abraham to take a paradoxical path. He was blessed, but without the visible signs of blessing: he received the promise that he would become a great people, but with a life marked by the barrenness of his wife Sarah; he was led to a new homeland but had to live there as a foreigner; and the only land he was permitted to possess was a lot in which to bury Sarah (cf. Gen 23:1–20). Abraham was blessed because in faith he was able to discern the divine blessing, going beyond appearances and trusting in God's presence even when God's paths seemed mysterious to him.

What does this mean to us? When we affirm "I believe in God", we are saying, like Abraham, "I trust in you, I entrust myself to you, O Lord", but not as Someone to whom to turn solely in times of difficulty or to whom to devote a few moments of the day or week. Saying "I believe in God" means founding my life on him, letting his Word guide it every day, in practical decisions, without fear of losing some part of myself. When, in the Rite of Baptism, the question is asked three times: "Do you believe?"—in God, in Jesus Christ, in the Holy Spirit, the holy Catholic Church, and the other truths of the faith, the triple response is in the singular: "I do", because it is my own life that with the gift of faith must be given a turning point, it is my life that must change, that must be converted. Every time we take part in a Baptism, we should ask ourselves how we ourselves live daily the great gift of faith.

Abraham the believer teaches us faith and, as a stranger on this earth, points out to us the true homeland. Faith makes us pilgrims on earth, integrated into the world and into history, but bound for the heavenly homeland. Believing in God thus makes us harbingers of values that often do not coincide with the fashion and opinion of the moment. It requires us to adopt criteria and assume forms of conduct that are not part of the common mind-set. Christians must not be afraid to go "against the current" in order to live their faith, resisting the temptation to "conform". In many of our societies, God has become the "great absent One", and many idols have supplanted him, multiform idols, especially possession and the autonomous "I". And even the major and positive breakthroughs of science and technology have instilled in people an illusion of omnipotence and self-sufficiency and an increasing egotism which has created many imbalances in interpersonal relations and social behavior.

Nevertheless, the thirst for God (cf. Ps 63[62]:1–2) has not been quenched, and the Gospel message continues to resonate in the words and deeds of numerous men and women of faith. Abraham, the father of believers, continues to be a father of many children who agree to walk in his footsteps and set out in obedience to the divine call, trusting in the benevolent presence of the Lord and receiving his blessing in order to become themselves a blessing for all. It is the blessed world of faith to which we are all called, in order to walk fearlessly, following the Lord Jesus Christ. And at times it is a difficult journey that also knows trial and death but that opens to life in a radical transformation of reality that only the eyes of faith can perceive and enjoy to the full.

Affirming "I believe in God" impels us, therefore, to set out, to come out of ourselves, exactly as Abraham did, to bring to the daily situation in which we live the certainty that comes to us from faith: namely, the certainty of God's presence in history today, too; a presence that brings life and salvation and opens us to a future with him for a fullness of life that will know no end.

15

"I believe in God, the Father Almighty"

WEDNESDAY, 30 JANUARY 2013
Paul VI Audience Hall

Dear Brothers and Sisters,

In last Wednesday's Catechesis we reflected on the opening words of the *Creed:* "I believe in God". But the Profession of Faith specifies this affirmation: God is the almighty Father, Creator of Heaven and earth. Thus I would like to reflect with you now on the first and fundamental definition of God which the Creed presents to us: he is Father.

It is not always easy today to talk about fatherhood, especially in the Western world. Broken families, an ever more absorbing workplace, the worry and often the struggle of families to make ends meet, and the distracting invasion of the media into our daily life: these are some of the many factors that can stand in the way of a calm and constructive relationship between father and child. At times communication becomes difficult, trust is lacking, and the relationship with the father figure can become problematic; moreover, in this way even imagining God as a father becomes problematic without credible models of reference. It is not easy for those who have experienced an excessively authoritarian

and inflexible father or one who was indifferent and lacking
in affection, or even absent, to think serenely of God and to
entrust themselves to him with confidence.

Yet the Revelation in the Bible helps us to overcome
these difficulties by speaking to us of a God who shows us
what it really means to be "father"; and it is the Gospel,
especially, which reveals to us this face of God as a Father
who loves, even to the point of giving his own Son for
mankind's salvation. The reference to the father figure thus
helps us to understand something of the love of God, which
is nevertheless infinitely greater, more faithful, and more
total than the love of any man. "What man of you", Jesus
asks in order to show the disciples the Father's face, "will
give his son a stone if he asks for bread? Or if he asks for a
fish, will give him a serpent? If you then, who are evil,
know how to give good gifts to your children, how much
more will your Father who is in heaven give good things
to those who ask him!" (Mt 7:9–11; cf. Lk 11:11–13). God
is our Father because he blessed us and chose us before the
creation of the world (cf. Eph 1:3–6); he has really made us
his children in Jesus (cf. 1 Jn 3:1). And as Father, God accompanies our lives with love, giving us his Word, his teaching,
his grace, and his Spirit.

As Jesus revealed—he is the Father who feeds the birds
of the air that neither sow nor reap and who arrays the
flowers of the field in marvelous colors, in robes more beautiful than those of Solomon himself (cf. Mt 6:26–32; Lk
12:24–28); and we, Jesus added, are worth far more than
the flowers and the birds of the air! And if he is so good
that he "makes his sun rise on the evil and on the good,
and sends rain on the just and on the unjust" Mt 5:45), we
shall always be able, without fear and with total confidence,
to entrust ourselves to his forgiveness as Father whenever

we err. God is a good Father who welcomes and embraces
his lost but repentant son (cf. Lk 15:11ff.), who gives freely
to those who ask him (cf. Mt 18:19; Mk 11:24; Jn 16:23),
and offers the bread of Heaven and the living water that
wells up to eternal life (cf. Jn 6:32, 51, 58).

Thus, although the person praying in Psalm 27 [26] is
surrounded by enemies and assailed by evildoers and slan-
derers, while seeking the Lord's help and invoking him, he
can bear his witness full of faith, as he states: "My father
and my mother have forsaken me, but the Lord will take
me up" (v. 10). God is a Father who never abandons his
children, a loving Father who supports, helps, welcomes,
pardons, and saves with a faithfulness that surpasses by far
that of men, opening onto dimensions of eternity. "For his
steadfast love endures for ever", as Psalm 136 [135] repeats
in every verse, as in a litany, retracing the history of salvation. The love of God the Father never fails, he does not
tire of us; it is a love that gives to the end, even to the
sacrifice of his Son. Faith gives us this certainty which
becomes a firm rock in the construction of our life: we can
face all the moments of difficulty and danger, the experience of the darkness of despair in times of crisis and suffering, sustained by our trust that God does not forsake us
and is always close in order to save us and lead us to eternal
life.

It is in the Lord Jesus that the benevolent face of the
Father, who is in Heaven, is fully revealed. It is in knowing him that we may also know the Father (cf. Jn 8:19;
14:7). It is in seeing him that we can see the Father, because
he is in the Father and the Father is in him (cf. Jn 14:9,11).
He is "the image of the invisible God", and, as the hymn
of the Letter to the Colossians describes him, he is: "the
first-born of all creation ... the first-born from the dead",

"in whom we have redemption, the forgiveness of sins" and the reconciliation of all things, "whether on earth or in heaven, making peace by the blood of his cross" (Col 1:13–20).

Faith in God the Father asks for belief in the Son, under the action of the Spirit, recognizing in the Cross that saves the definitive Revelation of divine love. God is our Father, giving us his Son; God is our Father, pardoning our sin and bringing us to joy in everlasting life; God is our Father, giving us the Spirit who makes us sons and enables us to call him, in truth, "Abba, Father!" (cf. Rom 8:15). It is for this reason that Jesus, teaching us to pray, invites us to say "Our Father" (Mt 6:9–13; cf. Lk 11:2–4).

Consequently, God's fatherhood is infinite love, tenderness that bends over us, frail children, in need of everything. Psalm 103 [102], the great hymn of divine mercy, proclaims: "As a father pities his children, so the Lord pities those who fear him. For he knows our frame; he remembers that we are dust" (vv. 13–14). It is our smallness, our frail human nature that becomes an appeal to the Lord's mercy, that he may show his greatness and tenderness as a Father, helping, forgiving us, and saving us.

And God responded to our plea by sending his Son, who died and rose for us; he entered our frailty and did what man on his own could never have done: as an innocent lamb, he took upon himself the sin of the world and reopened our path to communion with God, making us true children of God. It is there, in the Paschal Mystery, that the definitive face of the Father is revealed in its full splendor. And it is there, on the glorious Cross, that God's omnipotence as the "almighty Father" is fully manifested.

However, let us ask ourselves: How is it possible to think of an omnipotent God while looking at the Cross of Christ?

At this power of evil which went so far as to kill the Son of God? Naturally, what we would like would be a divine mightiness that fitted our own mind-set and wishes: an "omnipotent" God who solves problems, who intervenes to prevent us from encountering difficulties, who overcomes adverse powers, changes the course of events, and eliminates suffering. Thus today various theologians say that God cannot be omnipotent, for otherwise there would not be so much suffering, so much evil in the world. In fact, in the face of evil and suffering, for many, for us, it becomes problematic, difficult, to believe in a God who is Father and to believe that he is omnipotent; some seek refuge in idols, succumbing to the temptation to seek an answer in a presumed "magic" omnipotence and its illusory promises.

Nevertheless, faith in almighty God impels us to have a very different approach: to learn to know that God's thought is different from our own, that God's ways are different from ours (cf. Is 55:8), and that his omnipotence is also different. It is not expressed as an automatic or arbitrary force but is marked by a loving and paternal freedom. In fact, by creating free creatures, by giving us freedom, God renounced some of his power, allowing for the power of our freedom. Thus he loves and respects the free response of love to his call. As Father, God wishes us to become his children and to live as such in his Son, in communion, in full familiarity with him. His omnipotence is not expressed in violence, it is not expressed in the destruction of every adverse power, as we might like; rather, it is expressed in love, in mercy, in forgiveness, in accepting our freedom, and in the tireless call for conversion of heart, in an attitude only seemingly weak—God seems weak if we think of Jesus Christ who prays, who lets himself be killed. This apparently weak attitude consists of patience, meekness, and love; it shows that this is the real way to be powerful! This is God's power! And this power will win! The sage of the Book of Wisdom addressed God in these words: "For you are merciful to all, for you can do all things, and you overlook men's sins, that they may repent. For you love all things that exist.... You spare all things, for they are yours, O Lord who loves the living" (11:23–24a, 26).

Only those who are truly powerful can tolerate evil and show compassion; only those who are truly powerful can fully exercise the force of love. And God, to whom all things belong because all things were made by him, shows his power by loving everything and everyone, patiently waiting for the conversion of us men, whom he wants to be his children. God waits for our conversion. God's omnipotent love knows no bounds, to the extent that he "did not spare his own Son but gave him up for us all" (Rom 8:32). The omnipotence of love is not that of worldly power but is that of the total gift, and Jesus, the Son of God, reveals to the world the true omnipotence of the Father by giving his life for us sinners. This is the true, authentic, and perfect divine power: to respond to evil not with evil but with good, to insults with forgiveness, to homicidal hatred with life-giving love. Thus evil is truly vanquished because it is cleansed by God's love; thus death is defeated once and for all because it is transformed into a gift of life. God the Father raises the Son: death, the great enemy (cf. 1 Cor 15:26), is engulfed and deprived of its sting (cf. 1 Cor 15:54–55), and we, delivered from sin, can have access to our reality as children of God.

Therefore, when we say "I believe in God, the Father Almighty", we express our faith in the power of the love of God, who, in his Son, who died and was raised, triumphs over hatred, evil, and sin and unfolds before us the path to eternal life, as children who want to dwell forever in their "Father's House". Saying "I believe in God, the Father Almighty", in his power, in his way of being Father, is always an act of faith, of conversion, of the transformation of our thought, of the whole of our affection, of the whole of our way of life.

Dear brothers and sisters, let us ask the Lord to sustain our faith, to help us find true faith, and to give us the strength to proclaim the crucified and risen Christ and to witness to him in love of God and of neighbor. And may God grant that we accept the gift of our sonship, in order to live in fullness the reality of the Creed, in trusting abandonment to the love of the Father and to his merciful omnipotence, which is the true omnipotence and which saves.

16

"I believe in God: Maker of Heaven and earth, the Creator of man"

WEDNESDAY, 6 FEBRUARY 2013

Paul VI Audience Hall

Dear Brothers and Sisters,

The *Creed*, which begins by describing God as "the Father Almighty", the topic of our meditation last week, then adds that he is "Maker of Heaven and earth" and thus takes up the affirmation with which the Bible begins. Indeed, the first verse of Sacred Scripture reads: "In the beginning God created the heavens and the earth" (Gen 1:1). God is the origin of all things, and his omnipotence as a loving Father unfolds in the beauty of the creation.

In creation, God manifested himself as Father, since he is the origin of life, and in creating he shows his omnipotence. And Sacred Scripture uses very evocative images of it (cf. Is 40:12; 45:18; 48:13; Ps 104:2.5; 135:7; Prov 8:27–29; Job 38–39). As a good and powerful Father, he takes care of what he has created with unfailing love and faithfulness, as the Psalms say over and over again (cf. Ps 57:11; 108:5; 36:6). So it is that creation becomes a place in which to know and recognize the Lord's omnipotence and goodness as well as an appeal to our faith as believers so that we proclaim God as Creator. "By faith", the author of the Letter to the Hebrews wrote, "we understand that the world was created by the word of God, so that what is seen was made out of things which do not appear" (11:3). Faith thus implies the ability to recognize the invisible by identifying its traces in the visible world. Believers can read the great book of nature and understand its language (cf. Ps 19:2–5); but the Word of Revelation that awakens faith is necessary if man is to become fully aware of the reality of God as Creator and Father. The Book of Sacred Scripture says that human intelligence can find the clue to understanding the world in the light of faith. With the solemn presentation of the divine work of creation that unfolded over seven days, the first chapter of Genesis in particular occupies a special place. God brought the creation to completion in six days, and on the seventh, the Sabbath, he did not do anything, but rested: a day of freedom for all, a day of communion with God. Thus, with this image, the Book of Genesis tells us that God's first thought was to find a love that would correspond to his love. Then his second thought was to create a material world in which to place this love, these creatures who respond to him in freedom. This structure therefore results in the text being marked by certain meaningful repetitions. For example, the sentence "God saw that it was good" is repeated six times (vv. 4, 10, 12, 18, 21, 25) in order to conclude, the seventh time, after the creation of man: "God saw everything that he had made, and behold, it was very good" (v. 31). Everything that God creates is beautiful and good, steeped in wisdom and love; God's creative action brings order, instills harmony, and bestows beauty. In the narrative of Genesis, therefore, it becomes clear that the Lord created with his Word: ten times we read in the text the phrase: "God said" (vv. 3, 6, 9, 11, 14, 20, 24, 26,

28, 29). It is the Word, the *Logos* of God, who is at the origin of the reality of the world, and by saying: "God said", the effective power of the divine Word is emphasized. This is what the Psalmist sings: "By the word of the Lord the heavens were made, and all their host by the breath of his mouth . . . for he spoke, and it came to be, he commanded and it stood forth" (33[32]:6, 9). Life springs forth, the world exists, because all things obey the divine Word.

However, our question today is: In the age of science and technology, does speaking of creation still make sense? How should we understand the narratives in Genesis? The Bible does not intend to be a natural science manual; rather, it wishes to make the authentic and profound truth of things understood. The fundamental truth that the accounts of Genesis reveal to us is that the world is not a collection of forces that clash with each other; it has its origin and its permanence in the *Logos*, in God's eternal Reason, which continues to sustain the universe. A plan of the world exists which is conceived by this Reason, by the Creator Spirit. To believe that this is the foundation of all things illuminates every aspect of existence and gives us the courage to face the adventure of life with trust and hope. Therefore, Scripture tells us that the origin of being, of the world, our own origin, is not in the irrational or in need but, rather, in reason and love and freedom. Consequently, there is this alternative: either the priority of the irrational, of necessity, or the priority of reason, of freedom, of love. We believe in the latter hypothesis.

However, I would also like to say a word about the summit of all creation: man and woman, the human being, the only being "able to know and love his creator" (Pastoral Constitution on the Church in the Modern World, *Gaudium et Spes*, no. 12). Looking up at the heavens, the Psalmist wondered: "When I look at your heavens, the work of your fingers, the moon and the stars which you have established; what is man that you are mindful of him, and the son of man that you care for him?" (Ps 8:3–4). The human being, lovingly created by God, is indeed tiny in comparison with the immensity of the universe. At times, as we look with fascination at the enormous expanses of the firmament, we, too, perceive our limitations. Human beings are inhabited by this paradox: our smallness and our transience exist side by side with the greatness of what God's eternal love wanted for us.

The accounts of the creation in the Book of Genesis also usher us into this mysterious environment, helping us to become acquainted with God's plan for man. They affirm, first of all, that God formed man of dust from the ground (cf. Gen 2:7). This means that we are not God, we did not make ourselves, we are earth; yet it also means that we come from the good earth through the work of the good Creator. In addition, there is another fundamental reality: *all* human beings are dust, over and above the distinctions made by culture and by history, over and above every social difference; we are one humanity modeled with God's one earth. Then there is a second element: the human being came into existence because God breathed the breath of life into the body he had formed from earth (cf. Gen 2:7). The human being is made in God's image and likeness (cf. Gen 1:26–27). For this reason we all bear within us the life-giving breath of God and every human life—the Bible tells us—is under God's special protection. This is the most profound reason for the inviolability of human dignity against every attempt to evaluate the person according to utilitarian and power-based criteria. To be in the image and likeness of God indicates that man is not closed in himself but has in God an essential reference point.

In the first chapters of the Book of Genesis, we find two important images: the garden, with the tree of the knowledge of good and evil, and the serpent (cf. 2:15–17; 3:1–5). The garden tells us that the reality in which God has placed the human being is not a wild forest but a place that protects, nurtures, and sustains; and man must not consider the world as a property to be looted and exploited but as a gift of the Creator, a sign of his saving will, a gift to be cultivated and safeguarded, to increase and to develop with respect and in harmony, following its rhythms and logic in accordance with God's plan (cf. Gen 2:8–15). Then the serpent is a symbol that comes from the Oriental fertility cults that fascinated Israel and were a constant temptation to abandon the mysterious covenant with God. In this light, Sacred Scripture presents the temptation of Adam and Eve as the core of temptation and sin. What, in fact, did the serpent say? He did not deny God but insinuated a subtle question: "Did God say, 'you shall not eat of any tree of the garden'?" (Gen 3:1). This is how the serpent awoke in them the suspicion that the covenant with God was nothing but a chain that bound them, that deprived them of freedom and of the most beautiful and precious things of life. Their temptation became the temptation to build by themselves the world in which to live, to refuse to accept the limitations of being creatures, the limitations of good and evil, of morality; they saw their dependence on the love of God the Creator as a burden of which to free themselves. This is always the essence of temptation. But when the relationship with God is falsified, with a lie, putting ourselves in his place, all other relationships are altered. The other then becomes a rival, a threat. Straight after succumbing to the temptation, Adam turned on Eve (cf. Gen 3:12); the two conceal themselves from the sight of that God with whom they had been conversing as friends (cf. 3:8–10); the world is no longer the garden in which to live in harmony, but a place to exploit, riddled with hidden snares (cf. 3:14–19); envy and hatred for others entered man's heart. An example of this is Cain, who kills his own brother, Abel (cf. 4:3–9). Actually, in opposing their Creator, people go against themselves, deny their origin and, consequently, their truth; and evil, with its painful chain of sorrow and death, enters the world. More-over, all that God had created was good, indeed, very good, but after man opted freely for falsehood rather than truth, evil entered the world.

I would like to highlight a final teaching in the accounts of the creation; sin begets sin, and all the sins of history are interconnected. This aspect impels us to speak of what is called "original sin". What is the meaning of this reality, which is not easy to understand? I would just like to sug-gest a few points. First of all, we must consider that no man is closed in on himself, no one can live solely for him-self and by himself; we receive life from the other and not only at the moment of our birth but every day. Being human is a relationship: I am myself only in the "you" and through the "you", in the relationship of love with the "you" of God and the "you" of others. Well, sin is the distortion or destruction of the relationship with God; this is its essence: it ruins the relationship with God, the fundamental rela-tionship, by putting ourselves in God's place. The *Catechism of the Catholic Church* states that with the first sin man "chose himself over and against God, against the requirements of his creaturely status and therefore against his own good" (no. 398). Once the fundamental relationship is spoiled, the other relational poles are also jeopardized or destroyed: sin ruins relationships, thus it ruins everything, because we are relational. Now, if the relationship structure is disordered from the outset, every man comes into a world marked by this relational distortion, comes into a world disturbed by sin, by which he is marked personally; the initial sin tarnishes and wounds human nature (cf. *Catechism of the Catholic Church*, nos. 404–6).

And by himself, on his own, man is unable to extricate himself from this situation, on his own he cannot redeem himself; only the Creator himself can right relationships. Only if he from whom we distanced ourselves comes to us and lovingly holds out his hand can proper relationships be restored. This happens through Jesus Christ, who goes in exactly the opposite direction to Adam, as is described by the hymn in the second chapter of Saint Paul's Letter to the Philippians (2:5–11): whereas Adam did not acknowledge his creatural being and wanted to put himself in God's place, Jesus, the Son of God, was in a perfect filial relationship with the Father; he emptied himself and became the servant; he took the path of love, humbling himself even to death on a cross to set right our relations with God. The Cross of Christ thus became the new tree of life.

Dear brothers and sisters, living out faith means recognizing God's greatness and accepting our smallness, our condition as creatures, letting the Lord fill us with his love and thus develop our true greatness. Evil, with its load of sorrows and sufferings, is a mystery illuminated by the light of faith, which gives us the certainty that we can be freed from it: the certainty that it is good to be a human being.

APPENDIX

The Last General Audience of Pope Benedict XVI

WEDNESDAY, 27 FEBRUARY 2013
Saint Peter's Square

Venerable Brothers in the Episcopate and in the Presbyterate!
Distinguished Authorities!
Dear Brothers and Sisters,

I thank all of you for having come in such great numbers to this last General Audience.

Heartfelt thanks! I am truly moved, and I see the Church alive! And I think we should also say thanks to the Creator for the fine weather which he gives us even on this winter day.

Like the Apostle Paul in the biblical text which we have heard, I too feel a deep need first and foremost to thank God, who gives guidance and growth to the Church, who sows his word and thus nourishes faith in his people. At this moment, my heart expands and embraces the whole Church throughout the world; and I thank God for all that I have "heard" in these years of the Petrine ministry about faith in the Lord Jesus Christ and the love which truly circulates in the Body of the Church and makes it live in love and about the hope which opens and directs us toward the fullness of life, toward our heavenly homeland.

I feel that I bear everyone in prayer, in the present, God's present, in which I gather together every one of my meetings, journeys, and pastoral visits. In prayer I gather each and all, in order to entrust them to the Lord: that we might be filled with the knowledge of his will, with all spiritual wisdom and understanding, and that we might lead a life worthy of him and of his love, bearing fruit in every good work (cf. Col 1:9–10).

At this moment I feel great confidence, because I know, we all know, that the Gospel word of truth is the Church's strength, it is her life. The Gospel purifies and renews, it bears fruit, wherever the community of believers hears it and receives God's grace in truth and charity. This is my confidence, this is my joy.

When on 19 April, nearly eight years ago, I accepted the Petrine ministry, I had the firm certainty that has always accompanied me: this certainty of the life of the Church which comes from the Word of God. At that moment, as I have often said, the words which echoed in my heart were: Lord, why are you asking this of me, and what is it that you are asking of me? It is a heavy burden which you are laying on my shoulders, but if you ask it of me, at your word I will cast the net, sure that you will lead me even with all my weaknesses. And eight years later, I can say that the Lord has truly led me, he has been close to me, I have been able to perceive his presence daily. It has been a portion of the Church's journey which has had its moments of joy and light, but also moments which were not easy; I have felt like Saint Peter with the Apostles in the boat on the Sea of Galilee: the Lord has given us so many days of sun and of light winds, days when the catch was abundant; there were also moments when the waters were rough and the winds against us, as throughout the

Church's history, and the Lord seemed to be sleeping. But I have always known that the Lord is in that boat, and I have always known that the barque of the Church is not mine but his. Nor does the Lord let it sink; it is he who guides it, surely also through those whom he has chosen, because he so wished. This has been, and is, a certainty which nothing can shake. For this reason, my heart today overflows with gratitude to God, for he has never let his Church, or me personally, lack his consolation, his light, his love.

We are in the *Year of Faith*, which I desired precisely to reaffirm our faith in God in a context which seems to push him more and more into the background. I should like to invite all of us to renew our firm confidence in the Lord, to entrust ourselves like children in God's arms, certain that those arms always hold us, enabling us to press forward each day, even when the going is rough. I want everyone to feel loved by that God who gave his Son for us and who has shown us his infinite love. I want everyone to feel the joy of being a Christian. In one beautiful morning prayer, it says: "I adore you, my God, and I love you with all my heart. I thank you for having created me and made me a Christian. . . ." Yes, we are happy for the gift of faith; it is our most precious possession, which no one can take from us! Let us thank the Lord for this daily, in prayer and by a consistent Christian life. God loves us, but he also expects us to love him!

But it is not only God whom I want to thank at this moment. The Pope is not alone in guiding the barque of Peter, even if he is primarily responsible. I have never felt alone in bearing the joy and the burden of the Petrine ministry; the Lord has set beside me so many people who, with generosity and love for God and the Church, have helped me and been close to me. Above all, you, dear brother Cardinals: your wisdom, your counsel, and your friendship have been invaluable to me; my co-workers, beginning with my Secretary of State, who has faithfully accompanied me in these years; the Secretariat of State and the whole Roman Curia, as well as all those who in various sectors offer their service to the Holy See: many, many unseen faces which remain in the background, but precisely through their silent, daily dedication in a spirit of faith and humility they have been a sure and trustworthy support to me. I also think in a special way of the Church of Rome, my Diocese! I cannot forget my Brothers in the Episcopate and in the Presbyterate, the consecrated persons, and the entire People of God: in my pastoral visits, meetings, audiences, and journeys, I have always felt great kindness and deep affection; yet I, too, have felt affection for each and all without distinction, with that pastoral charity which is the heart of every Pastor, and especially of the Bishop of Rome, the Successor of the Apostle Peter. Every day I have borne each of you in prayer, with the heart of a father.

I would like my greeting and my thanksgiving to extend to everyone: the heart of the Pope reaches out to the whole world. And I wish to express my gratitude to the Diplomatic Corps accredited to the Holy See, which represents the great family of nations. Here I think, too, of all those who work for good communications, and I thank them for their important service.

At this point, I would also like to thank most heartily all those people throughout the world who in these recent weeks have sent me moving expressions of concern, friendship, and prayer. Yes, the Pope is never alone; now I once again experience this so overwhelmingly that my heart is touched. The Pope belongs to everyone, and so many persons feel very close to him. It is true that I receive letters from world leaders—from heads of state, from religious leaders, from representatives of the world of culture, and so on. But I also receive many, many letters from ordinary people, who write to me simply and from the heart and who show me their affection, an affection born of our being together with Christ Jesus, in the Church. These people do not write to me in the way one writes, for example, to a prince or some important person whom they do not know. They write to me as brothers and sisters, as sons and daughters, with a sense of a very affectionate family bond. Here one can sense palpably what the Church is—not an organization, an association for religious or humanitarian ends, but a living body, a communion of brothers and sisters in the Body of Christ, which makes us all one. To experience the Church in this way and to be able, as it were, to put one's finger on the strength of her truth and her love is a cause for joy at a time when so many people are speaking of her decline. But we see how the Church is alive today!

In these last months, I have felt my energies declining, and I have asked God insistently in prayer to grant me his light and to help me make the right decision, not for my own good, but for the good of the Church. I have taken this step with full awareness of its gravity and even its novelty, but with profound interior serenity. Loving the Church means also having the courage to make difficult, painful decisions, always looking to the good of the Church and not of oneself.

Here, allow me to go back once again to 19 April 2005. The real gravity of the decision was also due to the fact that from that moment on I was engaged always and forever by the Lord. Always—anyone who accepts the Petrine ministry no longer has any privacy. He belongs always and completely to everyone, to the whole Church. In a manner of speaking, the private dimension of his life is completely eliminated. I was able to experience, and I experience it even now, that one receives one's life precisely when one gives it away. Earlier I said that many people who love the Lord also love the Successor of Saint Peter and feel great affection for him; that the Pope truly has brothers and sisters, sons and daughters, throughout the world and that he feels secure in the embrace of your communion; because he no longer belongs to himself, he belongs to all and all belong to him.

The "always" is also a "forever"—there can no longer be a return to the private sphere. My decision to resign the active exercise of the ministry does not revoke this. I do not return to private life, to a life of travel, meetings, receptions, conferences, and so on. I am not abandoning the cross but am remaining in a new way at the side of the crucified Lord. I no longer bear the power of office for the governance of the Church, but in the service of prayer I remain, so to speak, in the enclosure of Saint Peter. Saint Benedict, whose name I bear as Pope, will be a great example for me in this. He showed us the way for a life which, whether active or passive, is completely given over to the work of God.

I also thank each and every one of you for the respect and understanding with which you have accepted this important decision. I will continue to accompany the Church's journey with prayer and reflection, with that devotion to the Lord and his Bride which I have hitherto sought to practice daily and which I would like to practice always. I ask you to remember me in prayer before God and, above all, to pray for the Cardinals, who are called to so weighty a task, and for the new Successor of the Apostle Peter: may the Lord accompany him with the light and strength of his Spirit.

Let us call upon the maternal intercession of the Virgin Mary, Mother of God and Mother of the Church, that she may accompany each of us and the whole ecclesial community; to her let us commend ourselves with deep confidence.

Dear friends! God guides his Church; he sustains her always, especially at times of difficulty. Let us never lose this vision of faith, which is the one true way of looking at the journey of the Church and of the world. In our hearts, in the heart of each of you, may there always abide the joyful certainty that the Lord is at our side: he does not abandon us; he remains close to us, and he surrounds us with his love.